THE WILDLIFE MAN

Barry Kaufmann-Wright

UPFRONT PUBLISHING
LEICESTERSHIRE

THE WILDLIFE MAN
Copyright © Barry Kaufmann-Wright 2001

ISBN 1 84426 026 7

First Published 2001 by
MINERVA PRESS

Second Edition 2002 by
UPFRONT PUBLISHING
Leicestershire

THE WILDLIFE MAN

Barry Kaufmann-Wright

All the events, incidents and cases within this book are true; however, the names in some have been changed.

Acknowledgements

To my wife Pat for her understanding and support in the writing of this book and the hours that she had to suffer my one-finger typing on a small portable typewriter.

To Julia Bryant, for painstakingly turning the original draft into legible English.

To Janie Stagg and Dave Smith, for their artistry.

To the estate of the late Gerald Durrell for allowing me to use the quotes in the chapter entitled 'Jersey Zoo'.

To Essex Police Press Office for the use of the photograph of myself with 'Bert'.

To Tony Eyles with grateful thanks for the cover photograph.

To my late grandfather, Tom Wright, for introducing me to the natural world so early in my life.

Contents

Memories of Childhood

My early childhood was spent on a small farm at Beaconview, Cheddington – an unpretentious village nestling at the north-eastern edge of the Chiltern Hills, with its main claim to fame being that it was the village where the Great Train Robbery occurred in the early 1960s.

The farm was a smallholding owned by my grandparents. It consisted of two houses – the farmhouse itself and a derelict keeper's cottage. The farmhouse, aptly named Beaconview, had a lovely view of Ivinghoe Beacon – a tall hill in part of the Chiltern chain of hills. The other cottage was adjacent to the Grand Union Canal that ran through the farm. The farm itself incorporated a poultry unit with over three thousand free-range chickens, ducks and geese. At night they were housed in old small-wheeled railway carriages that were dotted around the orchard and a large Nissen hut that my grandfather built near to Seabrook, the lock-keeper's cottage.

Barges, or what should properly be termed narrowboats, plied the canal and carried mainly coal and timber from Salford, Birmingham to Brentford, Middlesex, where the canal entered the River Thames. Most of these boats were diesel powered but many horse-drawn barges passed the farm, the large horses pulling the barges with apparent ease. The barges would have to pass though the lock that was about fifteen yards from Seabrook. My grandfather had a large iron lock key to open and shut the sluice gates on the lock in order to raise and lower the water levels. When I was old enough to be able to wind up the ratchet on the gates, I would open and close the lock myself. This meant that the 'bargees' did not need to leave their barges. They would sometimes throw me a tanner (sixpence in old money) but more often than not it was a smile and a wave. Sometimes they would moor up at the lock overnight. Occasionally they would sneak though the towpath hedge into the orchard and steal a chicken. The telltale signs were at the mooring post the following day – a big heap of feathers. What my grandfather would call them was unrepeatable but, of course, they were long gone by then.

I loved the canal and wildlife connected with it. I would spend hours there with our dog, Rex, a chocolate Labrador. We would just sit on the bank or on the lock gate, watching the world go by. Water voles would regularly swim across the canal and disappear into the vegetation on the other side for a short while, before swimming back. Swallows and house martins would drink by flying close to the water, with heads dropped and open beaks, skimming the surface. Black-headed gulls were regular visitors in the winter.

Rex and I would go off on long walks along the towpath. I would carry a shoulder bag containing marmite sandwiches and a drink, all of which I would share with my companion. We were often gone all day. One of Rex's favourite places was an old, rotten straw stack, which was quite a way from Beaconview. It was full of rodents, particularly rats, which Rex would chase but rarely caught. Kestrels, foxes, stoats and weasels would all hunt this veritable larder.

The southern side of the farm was bordered by the London Midland Scottish (LMS) railway line, which ran high up on an embankment. Steam trains thundered along this line day and night, spewing out their white smoke. At night one could often see red-hot coals coming out of the chimney and rolling down the embankment. In the summer they would often set light to the dry undergrowth. Occasionally these fires would get hold and spread along the embankment for some distance. My grandfather would regularly go up on to the embankment to collect unburned pieces of coal, so we always had plenty for the winter.

The embankment was another place that fascinated me for its wealth of wildlife; from rabbits that were everywhere to the buzzards that would fly high over the line hunting them. The small shrubs that tried to get a foothold on the embankment between the fires were full of birds, particularly in the summer with the migrants such as warblers and fly-catchers. It was my grandfather who explained migration to me and the reasons why these tiny birds fly for thousands of miles each year; I have always held a fascination for it. The sound of the willow warbler in April having flown up from Africa virtually non-stop, and that of the cuckoo in May, her-alded the balmy days of summer. House martins used to build their mud nests under the eaves of Seabrook, gather-ing mud from the murky pools around the farm. Swallows would also share the eaves there and one year I recall a pair actually nesting on a beam in one of the bedrooms of the cottage, flying in and out through a broken window over-looking the canal. By the autumn, they and their young had all departed for warmer climates, the mystique of migration.

The farm was surrounded by meadows for dairy cows, and in the field behind the Nissen hut there was a lovely pond, which had willow and alder trees down one side, with the side nearest Beaconview clear. During the summer, cat-tle would come and drink. This pond was full of life and I would spend many hours lying by the edge watching through the crystal-clear water: great crested newts in the early spring with their magnificent crests giving them the appearance of a miniature dinosaur; caddis fly larvae in their tube cases constructed of sand or twigs or a mixture, and bloodworms attached to the bottom of the pond; water scor-pions hunting the stickleback that abounded in the pond, the males in the spring with their bright red underparts chasing the drab females and building underwater nests for them; water beetles of many descriptions, including the huge carnivorous diving beetle, were regularly seen with their rear end protruding through the surface to take air. Sometimes they would emerge with a hapless stickleback held firmly in their jaws. Frogs and toads would breed in this pond and lay their eggs, the frogs in clumps and the toads in chains. I studied these and other pond life creatures for many hours, they taking little notice of Rex and I on the surface looking into their world. Rex would lie quite happily by my side, although he must have thought I was mad.

In the willow tree that overhung the orchard pond, a pair of little owls nested in a split base of one of the huge boughs. The adults were regularly seen hunting around the farm for insects. If I ventured too close to the nest, I would receive a fierce glare from the yellow eyes of the adult on guard. My grandfather taught me to respect nature and part of this important lesson was not to disturb nesting birds. With my first pair of binoculars, given to me by Santa Claus when I was five years old, I could watch birds and animals from a safe distance. I carried them everywhere with me, even on the walk along the country lane with its low hedges on the way to school.

I did, and still do, love the spring. With the arrival of summer migrants, the orchard used to resound to the glorious songs of the willow warbler, blackcap, chiffchaff and cuckoo, to name but a few. It would seem to burst into life with the birdsong and the emergence of the first leaves together with the beautiful blossoms of apple, pear and plum; the lovely shades of green as the trees slowly changed colour; the appearance of the first butterflies that had wintered as chrysalis. The brilliant yellow of the brimstone, the copper orange of the comma, the male orange tip with the deep orange gash on the end of its wing, the diminutive holly blue and later in the spring the tortoiseshell and peacock, all these butterflies would flutter amongst the tree blossom and the buttercups in the meadows.

Willow herb grew in the ditch that bordered our farm with the neighbours and I will always remember finding my first elephant hawk moth caterpillar on this plant. It was huge and monster-like to my child's eye. Big, fat and grey with a large eye marking at one end, I was convinced it was poisonous but, of course, it wasn't. Despite my fear of it, I managed to get the caterpillar into a jam jar, along with the plant, and take it back to the house to show Gran. She was not at all amused and told me to return it to where I had found it. I did this and watched in fascination and awe as it crawled lethargically back into the depths of the plant. I had checked its identity in my Observers' book of *Butterflies and Moths*. I had the entire series of these little books covering every aspect of nature and I learned a tremendous amount from them. (It was some years later before I saw my first elephant hawk moth.)

The autumn was fruit picking time and was a busy period of the year for us. We helped our neighbours and in return they allowed us to store our fruit in their cellar. I remember the huge influx of red admiral butterflies that fed in their hundreds on the windfall fruit. Wasps were everywhere and I developed an early respect for them, especially after what happened to my sister Corinne and her friend. The wasps would normally build their beautiful nests either in holes in the ground or in the trees and would feed on the fruit around them; the Victoria plums were by far their favourite. Corinne and her friend were in the orchard one autumn, near the pond. She would have been four or five years old at this time. They were talking as girls do at this age whilst, quite innocently, throwing small stones at the large willow tree that overhung the pond from the opposite bank to where they were standing. Grandad and I were in the orchard working when suddenly out of the tree fell what I can only describe as a ball of wasps which immediately attacked the two girls without mercy. I will never forget their screams as we rushed over to try and help them. In the frenzy I received stings to my hands but Corinne got the worst of the wasps' anger with over thirty stings. In her desperation to get away, and screaming in agony, she swallowed some, which continued to sting as they went down. This had the effect of closing her windpipe. Corinne was rushed to hospital along with her friend who had not been stung as badly. They both survived the ordeal, Corinne for one, with a deep respect (fear) of these creatures.

Once all the fruit had been gathered in, it was stored in boxes in the cellar of our neighbour's farmhouse. This cellar held a fascination for me. It was deep and dark, like a dungeon to a small child. Grandad and I would often go down into its depths to move boxes or load them on to his Bedford Dormobile ready for market. I can still taste the strong, sweet, pungent smell of rotting, as, inevitably, some bruised fruit would eventually perish.

The boxes were stored on thin, raised wooden slats, allowing air to circulate and keeping them dry. This half-inch gap between the box and the floor was a perfect space for great crested newts to hibernate through the winter. It was an ideal spot for them – dark, damp and frostproof. When the bottom box was lifted off the slats, there would be literally hundreds of these beautiful black, nine-inch long creatures coiled up virtually on top of each other. They made no attempt to move. Even if I picked one up they remained in their rigid coil. Their bright yellow and black undersides were very distinctive. Within a day or so of being disturbed they had moved under another box. Fortunately for them there were always a few boxes left well into the spring, when these amphibians would leave the cellar and migrate to their breeding ponds. It was always a mystery how they got in and out of the cellar. I have never seen such a heavy concentration of great crested newts since.

These newts, along with their more common cousins, would often get into the well outside Seabrook, which supplied water to Beaconview. These newts and other creatures would regularly be pumped through to the kitchen sink by using a wooden-handled pump adjacent to the sink. I used to take them out of the sink and release them in the orchard, apparently none the worse for a ride along the pipes. When Grandad removed the wooden lid to the well, newts would be perched in crevices down the well walls, particularly in the summer when the water level was low. Like the cellar, it was a mystery how they got in and out. Even the occasional frog would be seen swimming happily around, although I must say I never saw one in the sink.

Early autumn was another busy period with the harvest. Although we did not grow cereals ourselves, Grandad helped our neighbours. In those days, farmers and farm workers helped each other out when labour demands were great and these harvests were before the days of combines on every farm. Our neighbours, the Kinghams, still cut and stacked the wheat in the field as sheaves or stooks. These were collected on low trailers and were often stacked fifteen feet high, being thrown up on the end of long-handled pitchforks. Back at the farm they were offloaded and stacked in huge ricks ready for the threshing machine. This massive machine would then be parked next to the ricks and two men, one often being Grandad, would then untie the sheaves by cutting the string, allowing the wheat to fall into the machine where it was separated from the straw. A huge belt that went on to a large green tractor with a flywheel on one side drove the threshing machine. I used to call this the 'Pom Pom' tractor because when it was running it made that deep sound. Other men were engaged in removing the heavy sacks of grain. The chaff and straw were carried on an elevator away from the machine and dropped some distance away. It was hot, dusty work but a magical time for me. I used to sit under the machine near to where the chaff would drop. This was long before the days of Health and Safety. The reason I sat there was to catch the tiny little harvest mice that would drop out of the machine. None were injured or the worse for their ordeal of passing through the machine. I would collect them in jam jars, feed them some grain that they readily accepted and watch them for a while before releasing them into the safety of the field.

The noise and dust from the huge machine was incredible. Rex used to spend his time with the farm's Jack Russell terriers, catching rats that used to teem out of the rick. Despite the huge rodent numbers, none got away. Even the farm cats joined in the foray. Many of these were feral and there was one in particular that I will always remember. He was a large black and white tomcat with a broken and folded right ear. He was as big as a corgi and very heavily built. His head was very broad and he had long white whiskers, whilst his front legs were bowed like a bulldog. He would spend the summer in the fields around the farm and would only come in for the threshing. In deep winter he would be seen around the farm. Many of the cats and kittens in the area were black and white and had similar markings to him but, of course, I did not realise the significance of this until I was a little older. The other farmyard cats showed him a great deal of respect and even the dogs kept their distance. He was very much like a character out of a Disney cartoon with a real personality.

Nan used to bring out sandwiches for everyone, with cider for the men and orange juice for me. When I was a little older I was allowed on top of the rick to pitch the stooks to Grandad on the machine and I thought this was great. At the end of the threshing, Mr Kingham used to give me half a crown, which was an absolute fortune to me. I used to go straight up to the village shop and buy blackjacks and fruit salads at four for a penny. Needless to say, I didn't spend much of the 2s 6p (approximately 25p in new money).

When I was five years old, I started primary school at Cheddington. My cousin Simon who lived at the other end of the village started at the same time but, unlike him, I did-n't like school very much, especially after the freedom of the farm. However, I slowly settled in, particularly after we began the nature study class. The BBC started a short school series, I believe it was called *Nature Time* and despite it being in black and white, I thought it was fabulous. I was totally absorbed. The programme was supplemented with a black and white magazine and this was my main help when learn-ing to read. At home I started watching such programmes as *Zoo Quest* with David Attenborough, whom I was later to meet, Armand and Michaela Denis on safari in Africa, Hans and Lotti Hass under the sea, and George Cansdale with ani-mals in the studio. I also met him later in life when it was I who gave a talk and our roles were reversed. All these people were to have a profound influence on me in my early years and later Desmond Morris with *Zoo Time*, Gerald Durrell and Graham Dangerfield continued this influence.

I eventually settled into school life but always enjoyed the walk home down a little country road from the village, which led to the farm. In the summer the low roadside hedges on either side were full of birds. Yellow hammers would perch at the top of the hedge singing their song 'A lit-tle bit of bread and no cheese'. Whether it was sunny or rain-ing, they were there. Skylarks would sing high above and it was a good eyesight test to try and spot these tiny birds in the blue summer sky. In the winter the hedges housed redwings and fieldfares, which lunched on the hedgerow berries. These birds had flown down from Greenland and Russia. Hips and haws, sloes and crab apples were all devoured by huge flocks of these birds. I would endeavour to count them but always ran out of fingers.

I remember finding a wren's nest in the ivy that was creeping up the wall of the railway bridge that spanned the lane leading to the farm. Every day on the way home from school I would stop on the opposite side of the lane to the nest and watch as the adults would fly into the nest with beaks full of insects for their developing young. I could not believe the frequency of the visits. Where did they find these insects so quickly? At weekends I would sit for hours, and one Saturday afternoon I was privileged to witness the chicks, which were miniatures of their parents, fledge the nest. I could see the beaks at the tiny round entrance of the nest that was constructed of moss, and on occasions a head would appear as an adult arrived with yet more insects.

Shortly after one of the adults had left, suddenly without any warning, a chick left the nest and jumped on to a nearby branch. It seemed to be surveying the wonders of the world outside, tipping its head from side to side and taking in the new shapes and sounds. This fledgling was joined shortly by another, then another and another until there were eight fledglings in a row along the branch. I previously had no idea how many babies were in the nest but the final tally astonished me. It was impossible to believe that this number had come out of such a tiny nest. What a wonderful photo it would have made! The parents were frantically calling them from my side of the lane and one by one they took their maiden flights. These appeared very precarious, particularly when landing in the hedge a few yards from where I was standing.

The last one to fly misjudged it completely and landed at my feet. I wanted to bend down and pick it up but I remembered being told by Grandad that you should never handle young birds. Almost immediately one of the adults flew past me, scolding me severely, and I moved away from the chick and stood under the bridge. I turned just in time to see the chick flying up into the hedge to join its siblings. I rushed home to tell Nan and Grandad what I had seen. I dragged Grandad down to the bridge to show him the nest but the birds had disappeared by this time. I later learned that wrens will often have more than one clutch in a season, but this pair did not reuse the nest in the ivy that year, much to my disappointment.

It was when I turned six years old that I saw my first fox, and a magnificent animal it was too. I was walking along the tow-path on my own, Rex being lame with a thorn in his foot. It was a beautiful morning with the sunlight flickering on the surface of the water as the gentle breeze rippled the reflection. I had walked on past the Ivinghoe Road and there was a clear view of the Beacon Hill to my right. I was about to sit near the water's edge to eat my marmite sandwiches, when suddenly from the hedge about twenty yards ahead of me a fox leapt on to the towpath. We both stared at each other in total disbelief. It was an adult with a wide head, a long-flowing brush with a white tip. The red coat appeared to shine in the sun as the breeze ruffled it. His broad white chest was tinged with grey around the edges. This was one of those magical moments that, even at my tender age, I could appreciate. There we were, totally transfixed.

I was convinced that at any moment he would disappear as quickly as he had come. I don't know who was more surprised and I was just glad that Rex was not with me for once. The fox flicked his ears and sniffed the air in my direction but fortunately the breeze was in my face, therefore taking my scent away from him. He twitched his tail like a cat. I don't recall how long the brief encounter lasted. I was standing perfectly still, motionless, hardly breathing. It was as if he almost knew I wasn't posing a threat to him, but was not quite certain. His wariness was understandable and he hadn't reached maturity by taking chances. Suddenly, as quickly as he had appeared, he turned back and went through the hedge. I rushed forward to get one more glimpse of him but he was gone. I ran home to tell Grandad, although I knew he detested foxes for the threat they posed to the poultry. I was right, he did not share my enthusiasm but, despite this attitude, it was an encounter I was never to forget.

As with the fox, my first experience with a badger was one that was to leave a lasting impression on me, and this time I shared it with Rex. We had endured one of those long, hot, dry summers and there were many scorched patches along the embankment. One autumn evening, Rex and I were out walking. We had been over the swing bridge across the canal and were walking along the fence below the embankment. Cows were grazing in the setting sunlight, many lying down chewing the cud. Suddenly, I spotted a black and white form on the other side of the field under the hedge. It appeared to be moving slowly through the grass, which was short from the heavy grazing and lack of rain. I immediately put Rex on his lead and crouched down. Rex thought this was a great game and started licking my face. I was trying to watch the badger and, as with the fox, I was mesmerised, but this time the badger was not aware of my presence. Rex eventually gave up the game and lay down, unaware of what I was watching.

The badger was searching for food and was turning over

old, dried cowpats, some of which it was tearing apart with its feet and mouth. It appeared to be getting morsels from this activity. I later learned that they get worms and grubs from under and within the cowpats. It was a lovely clear evening, swallows were flying low over the field, weaving in and out of the cows and gathering the last of the summer's insects before their long journey. The badger was moving from pat to pat and slowly away from the hedge in our direction. We were about one hundred yards from it with three or four prone cows between us. There was no breeze and little chance of it picking up our scent.

We sat quite motionless and I suspect that Rex thought I was quite mad. He even remained quiet when a hedgehog appeared from the undergrowth ahead of us and snuffled out into the field, having skirted around where we were. Its purpose appeared to be the same as the badger, although it was moving a lot faster. It did stop once or twice to pick up something but it eventually disappeared in the undergrowth behind us. I had seen hedgehogs before in the orchard and my attention returned to the badger. I don't know how long I watched him, but when he eventually left through the hedge, the harvest moon was rising above the Ivinghoe Beacon. I was late to bed that night but it had been worth it – another fantastic experience. In my certainty of the badger returning, I dragged Grandad out to the field the next night but, of course, it did not show. Grandad did tell me that many years ago, long before I was born, he had seen one in the orchard at night. I spent a long time after that searching for the badger's sett but without success. Some time later I learned that there was a massive and well-established sett in the spinney on the side of the hill across the field from the end of our farm lane.

My brief encounter with the badger was the beginning of a lifelong interest in these fascinating animals. One characteristic I learned about them is that they travel great distances in search of food; the spinney sett was about a mile from where I had first seen my badger.

Another encounter involving a nuthatch was of significance in my life. One or two of the trees in the orchard were old and split, in particular one ancient Victoria plum tree. This had a deep crevice down the trunk but despite this, it produced copious amounts of the most delicious plums. I was in the orchard one day with my head just above the cow parsley when I noticed a curious blue/grey bird descending the trunk of the plum tree, after which it disappeared into the crack. I could see something at the bottom but could not readily make out what it was. I thought nothing more of it but as I walked away, the bird reappeared with what looked like mud in its beak and down into the crack it went. I went home and consulted my Observers' book of *Birds* and there it showed a nuthatch. I continued to watch the tree for several days afterwards and it became obvious that the pair were building a nest deep down in the trunk of the tree.

Two or three weeks later I was again watching the adults bringing insects to the nest. Even with a torch I could hardly see much of the construction deep inside but I was certain there were young there due to the copious amounts of insects that the adult pair were bringing at two-minute intervals. Although I was hidden in the cow parsley, I am sure the adults knew I was there. Each day I would rush home from school and straight out to the orchard to see what they were up to. Eventually the young fledged the nest and once again I was privileged to see the four young perched high up in the plum tree just after they had made their maiden voyage into the outside world. The fruit trees seemed to provide an ample supply of food to these interesting birds and they could often be seen descending the boughs and tree trunks.

High summer in the meadow behind the Nissen hut brought a blaze of colour with the flowering of the buttercups and daisies. The pond would have hundreds of baby great crested newts swimming in the shallows, the adults would be leaving the water having cast their spectacular mating costumes. Tadpoles of frogs and toads were developing legs ready for their terrestrial stage. The water scorpions and diving beetles were reducing the numbers of all three as they took full advantage of the food bonanza.

I developed a healthy respect for the larval stage (nymphs) of dragonflies. As these grew in the water, their prey grew proportionally larger. They would take tadpoles, fish and, if food was in short supply, each other. I once caught one in a net and made the big mistake of removing it by hand. It bit hard into my finger with its powerful jaws and, boy, did that hurt. (Hence the healthy respect.) I watched a nymph climb a piece of bulrush that was projecting out of the water. Once clear of the water, it stopped climbing and remained quite still. I had a good view, being only a few feet away, and watched in fascination as its back split open and the adult dragonfly emerged over the course of a few minutes. The dragonfly stretched out its wings in the sun and flew off, leaving behind the empty carcass of its nymph form.

This was my first introduction to metamorphosis – one of life's fascinating features. During another occasion when I was lying prone on the ground peering into the pond, I looked up to see an adult black and yellow striped dragonfly hovering literally within three feet of my face with its large eyes fixed on me. It seemed to hang there for ages as if sizing me up as a tasty morsel, but after deciding I was too big, it flew off.

This pond, along with the one in the orchard, was visited by a number of birds including the mallard duck, moorhen and heron. Each summer, a pair of spotted flycatchers nested in the willow tree overhanging the orchard pond, whilst a kingfisher would regularly visit the meadow pond and the canal to catch stickleback. A pair of little owls nested in a crack in one of the meadow pond willows, and they seemed to get used to my presence. They could often be seen on the ground picking up insects and worms for their three owlets. One of these died, but two fledged the nest successfully; sadly I found the other one dead in the canal shortly afterwards. I can only assume that it fell into the water, as the tree that the nest was in was near the towpath.

On the surface of the meadow pond there floated pond skaters and whirligig beetles that rippled the water as they spun around furiously. I could not understand why they did not sink. Grandad tried to explain water tension to me but it was beyond my comprehension at the time. The predatory pond skaters would gather round hapless flies or other unfortunate insects that had fallen on to the water surface, and suck the juices from them. Nature shows no mercy.

With the two ponds and the canal, it is no wonder that I have always held a deep fascination for water life, both above and below the surface.

It was in these early years that I rapidly learned the harsh realities of man's coexistence with nature, along with the realisation that nature can be cruel and uncompromising. Any sick or injured poultry that Grandad found and which he thought might respond to a little tender loving care, he would give to me to look after. I had a small pen in the orchard with a hutch for the birds to roost in at night. Grandad provided the food and I supplied the time. I used to let the birds out and feed them before leaving for school, and would shut them in before I went to bed. I had a reasonable success rate and the activity also gave me valuable experience at caring for birds, which was to prove very useful in later life.

One summer I was caring for a lot of birds, including a cockerel with a torn wattle, a lame chicken and some ducklings that had been orphaned. I had shut them up one night and secured the clasp on the door with the wire as usual. The following morning, I was up at the crack of dawn to feed them before I went to school. I will never forget the scene that greeted me as I approached the pen. The pen itself, which was quite a solid structure, was on its side and the door was open. I rushed back to the house and dragged Grandad out. When we returned to the pen, I found the remains of one of the ducklings some way off, then another and the head of a third. Grandad came across the headless corpse of the cockerel but there was no sign of the lame hen. Grandad tried to explain that it was more than likely the work of a fox, but I was crying uncontrollably. At eight years old I could not understand, or comprehend, what had happened at all. Why had the fox killed everything but apparently only taken one hen? I cried for most of the morning at school and Grandad collected me at lunch time.

That night Grandad was convinced that the fox would return and he decided to set a trap for it. After nagging him, he rather reluctantly agreed that I could go along. He placed the carcass of the cockerel in the orchard near the pond and close to an empty hen house. A light on the side of the Nissen hut cast a dull glow across the orchard and the dead cockerel. Grandad's plan was to sit in the empty hen house and wait with his gun. We sat there peering out through a slit, Grandad holding the double-barrelled shotgun in his large hands. I had seen the gun on many occasions, but had never been with Grandad when he actually fired it. The barrels glinted in the moonlight. A tawny owl hooted close by; it sounded as though it were on the roof of the hen house we were sitting in. It seemed like hours that we crouched, waiting, unable to move, as the floorboards creaked with every movement.

Suddenly I spotted a fox moving in from our left. I grabbed Grandad's arm but he had already seen it. The fox was sniffing the air as it homed in on the cockerel. As it came into full view, I was struck with the thought that this beautiful creature was about to die and then my mind flashed back to the carnage of that morning. Even at that early age I had very mixed emotions. The fox approached the cockerel, and as it did so, Grandad slowly raised up the gun, poking the barrels through the gap in the hen house. He took aim and, as the fox was about to pick up the bird, fired both barrels almost simultaneously. The noise in the hut was unbelievable and my ears were ringing for a long time afterwards. My body was trembling, as the fox dropped like a stone. We left the hut and walked over to where the fox lay covered in blood. Grandad picked it up by its brush and said that it was a vixen with cubs.

A wave of remorse came over me as we had killed a mother and the cubs would now die too. I went straight to bed when I got home. I lay on my bed staring at the ceiling. I could not stop thinking about the cubs and the fact that the vixen had lost her life trying to feed her family. Tears flowed and it became impossible to reconcile the loss of my birds with the loss of the cubs. I overheard Grandad and Gran talking downstairs and will always remember the comment that Grandad made that, 'It's a tough lesson for him to learn, but learn he must.' It *was* a hard time but as I grew older I realised that nature can be beautiful, fascinating and spectacular as well as harsh and cruel. After the shooting, I spent several frantic days searching for the earth to try and save the cubs. I believe that Grandad knew what I was up to but he did not interfere. I was unsuccessful but I never forgot that incident.

Another episode that brought home to me the harshness of nature came about when we had returned to the farm after my mother had completed another housekeeping job. At the time I had two beautiful rabbits, Whisky, a brown doe, and Soda, a silver doe. I thought the world of them. I had brought their hutch back but Grandad had already made me a much bigger one. We placed it to the side of the sitting room window that overlooked the orchard. There was a large cherry tree in front of the window that provided shade for the rabbits from the early morning sun. Their new hutch was on legs, to keep it well clear of the ground, and Grandad had also built a run for them to play in during the day. The rabbits soon settled in and I was really pleased to be back at the farm and school at Cheddington. Rex and I searched out all our regular haunts, including the old straw rick. He was fascinated with my rabbits and when they were in the run they would hop over and sniff Rex and he would sniff them back. He never once threatened them and I think he realised that they were very special.

Life carried on as normal but it was soon to be thrown into turmoil once again due to the natural world. The rabbits had been in their run all day whilst I was at school. I threw them some fresh grass when I got home and later put them back in the hutch, which I padlocked – a lesson learned from the fox incident. I woke early as usual the following morning, washed and dressed and went to put the rabbits in the run, saving breakfast until later. What I saw outside was totally devastating. Both rabbits were dead and there was blood everywhere. I rushed indoors and returned with Mum and Nan in tow. I was crying uncontrollably and couldn't believe it. Grandad had left early to deliver the eggs and it was decided to leave the hutch as it was until he returned. I walked to school, still sobbing. The headmaster, Mr Hawkins, decided to send me home at morning break as I was crying incessantly, and so Grandad came to pick me up. He had disposed of the remains of the two rabbits and on clearing out all the dishevelled bedding he had found a hole chewed through the floor of the hutch about one and a half inches in diameter. It was the work of a stoat. For a long time afterwards I thought of the terror that the rabbits must have experienced as this fierce hunter had entered the hutch. I did not keep rabbits again, despite Grandad's offer to buy me some.

I had my own first-hand experience with a stoat some time later. I was at Mentmore with my cousin Simon, on the other side of Cheddington to our farm. We were walking along the straight lane that leads to the 'Towers' when I spotted a stoat lying on the side. Without thinking I picked it up and to my surprise it was still alive, although the amount of blood on it suggested otherwise. Before I had a chance to react, it had sunk its jaw into my left thumb muscle. The pain was unbelievable. My immediate reaction was to pull it away, which I did, but the animal's jaws remained firmly shut and it ripped out a large piece of the muscle and the blood flowed freely. Very little traffic used this lane but luck had not totally deserted me. A lady stopped and ran me home. Grandad took me to the hospital where they managed to sew my hand up but I still have the scar to this day. The stoat died shortly afterwards from its injuries. Another lesson had been learned the hard way – do not pick up an apparently dead animal until you have established that it is definitely dead!

Winter was often a hard time on the farm. During snow and sub-zero temperatures, the poultry were locked in the houses dotted around the orchard but the majority were kept in the Nissen hut, the tiered perches meaning that they were off the ground and relatively warm. The hut could hold over two thousand birds and the winter inevitably created additional work with extra feeding and cleaning out. I used to rush home and change quickly in order to get out and help Grandad. Homework – what was that? I think that my primary school gave up on me eventually.

The main food for the poultry was a mix of bran, wheat and maize along with anything else that was around, particularly potatoes. All this was mixed together in a large galvanised bath. I used to roll my sleeves up and get stuck in, kneeling on a high stool to reach. A lot of water was then poured in, which turned the mixture into a mash. In the winter the mash was fed to the poultry in their respective houses, but in the spring and summer they were fed in long troughs outside Seabrook, by the well cover. Having filled the troughs, Grandad would whistle, a type of 'Whow whow whow whow' starting very high and transcending to a lower pitch. I can only liken the noise to the call of a willow warbler. The birds would recognise it immediately and rush over, the chickens running so fast that they were almost flying with their wings flapping madly. I am certain that the geese really did fly!

It looked quite awesome to see three thousand birds of all shapes and sizes descending on the troughs, mainly from the direction of the orchard. A feeding frenzy then followed. Starlings would arrive to grab the odd morsel but they seemed to spend more time squabbling amongst themselves than actually feeding. As the poultry finally dispersed, other birds joined in including jackdaws, magpies and the secretive little dunnock that crept in between the troughs, picking up a mouthful unnoticed by the bigger birds that strutted around. In the early autumn we were sometimes hosts to the winter visitors, redwings and fieldfares, who would sometimes go to the troughs but were more likely to visit the orchard to feed on the windfall fruit.

I used to enjoy the arrival of the snow that made tracking great fun. It was amazing how many animals came by the orchard. Foxes, hares and rabbits all left their tracks in the soft snow. If it came in really hard, school was closed. This was great because it meant that I could put on my wellington boots and go off tracking with Rex. He loved the snow and would bound along with his head down using his nose like a plough. I remember once tracking a fox through the orchard and the towpath hedge. Keeping Rex by my side, we followed the track along the towpath and under the railway bridge. The track was lost under the bridge as there was no snow but it continued the other side. The snow on the path was not very deep as it was protected by the hedge; however, where the snow had been blown through the small holes in the base of the hedge, snow sculptures had been created, resembling mountains with long straight sharp ridges. Where the hedge was thin and full of holes, the sculptures were more like a mountain range. Although these were quite deep, the fox did not appear to have had any difficulty in walking through them.

The snow was coming over the top of my boots. We continued under the humpback bridge and passed the Duke of Wellington pub on the opposite bank. The light was beginning to fade and the grey sky was heavy with more snow. There were a few barges moored up and they looked strange with their snowy blankets. Lights were on inside the boats and smoke was billowing from the chimneys. We walked past them, still heading towards Long Marston and Tring. The wind was beginning to pick up and the snow started to fall again. We continued although the track of the fox was beginning to fade. The wind was now starting to pick up the snow lying on the ground and the falling snow was becoming heavier. Suddenly the track left the path and went through a hole in the hedge across the field towards the spinney on the hill. With the light rapidly fading and the wind and snow increasing, I decided to trek back to the farm. By the time we had reached the gate into the farm from the towpath, the falling snow was horizontal and was mixing with the snow being picked up in the gale force wind. My navy blue duffle coat was now white and so was Rex, his long whiskers drooping with ice. Inevitably, I was plonked straight into a bath when I reached the farmhouse.

The following day the full extent of the blizzard could be seen. The snow was level with the top step outside the back door. Rex took one look and leapt headlong into the snow before promptly disappearing. I followed him and the snow came up to my waist – boy, this was fun! Rex resurfaced and went bounding off, leaping up and crashing down – he loved it! He was a powerful dog and I had great difficulty in keeping up with him. The sun was shining and the snow glistened. I started throwing snowballs at Rex who would try to catch them. Sometimes his entire head would turn white as the snowball exploded in his face. He would be unfazed, simply shaking his head and wagging his tail whilst waiting for the next one. He would sometimes leap out of the snow in his efforts to catch the incoming snowball and obviously had great fun. After helping Grandad feed the poultry, Rex and I went into the orchard. Shafts of sunlight were cascading through the trees and the snow-laden boughs were shedding their white covering. Once or twice when these fell on Rex, he would shake himself and look at me with a big smile on his face.

The cold spell lasted for a week or more and, of course, there was no school. Rex and I were up at the crack of dawn and, after helping with the poultry, we were off across the fields. We saw a double steam train clearing the track with a huge snowplough on the front of the lead tender. Plumes of white smoke billowed from their funnels and rolled down the embankment. We found many tracks on the towpath from moorhen to heron, fox, hare and water vole.

One morning we had walked beyond the Ivinghoe Road and under the bridge when I found a track that I had never seen before. It was large and rounded with webbed toes and was four-footed. The track came through a hole in the hedge and almost immediately wandered out on to the ice on the canal before disappearing into the water in the middle. There was ice on either side with an open channel down the middle. I checked my books when I went home and decided it was an otter. I told Grandad my theory but he dismissed it. I was convinced I was right but never found the track again after the snow thawed.

The thaw came quickly and the canal level rose rapidly resulting in the bank in front of Seabrook bursting, releasing the ice cold water, which cascaded down into the farm. The orchard flooded and although the farmhouse was on slightly higher ground, the water was up to the bottom step. The snow had been great fun but this was not. British Waterways were rapidly sent for to repair the bank and the water soon subsided from the farm, leaving the pond and all the ditches full. As the flood water subsided, it left in its wake a tragedy. Hundreds of dead fish swept out of the canal in the flood water were all over the farm. There were corpses of bream, carp, tench, gudgeon, perch and many other species. I will always remember the menacing eye of a large pike that I found near the Nissen hut; even in death it was threatening. Grandad gave me the job of gathering them all up in a wheelbarrow before they were dumped in a corner of the orchard. We put a bale of straw over them and set fire to it. Grandad also had to pump the well dry as it had filled with canal water.

The snow and the flooding had all occurred in December, which was in itself a busy time for Grandad with the Christmas poultry market. The Kingham brothers, from our neighbouring farm, would come over and give a hand with the plucking. I had learned to pluck and draw a chicken, but for every one that I finished, the others were managing three. The birds then went to supply many of the local butchers and a lot were sold at market.

The following March, after the snow and flood, we were to experience the effect of another elemental force. When I had come home from school, a strong westerly wind was blowing. White clouds were racing across the blue sky and the wind appeared to be getting stronger by the hour. After tea I helped Grandad lock the chickens up. There were several broody bantams sitting on eggs in the new arks that Grandad had put up in the orchard. There were also about one hundred chicks under a lamp in a pen in Seabrook. Having checked on all those, I went to bed and Grandad forecast that we were in for a rough night. That was an understatement. By midnight the wind was really howling outside. I lay in bed listening to the noise. At the height of the gale it was one continual roar. There was a loud crash from the direction of the orchard followed by another immediately below my window as a roof tile shattered. Out of my window I could see the big willow at the end of the Nissen hut swaying backwards and forwards as the wind tossed it in all directions. Another crash from the orchard and the sound of splitting wood. I slept very little that night.

The following morning revealed the full extent of devastation that the gale had left in its path. Outside the back door were the remains of two of the ridge tiles from the roof. The scene that greeted us in the orchard was unbelievable. One of the new arks had blown over but miraculously the hens that had been inside were quite happily scratching around outside. Unfortunately, a clutch of eggs that a broody hen had been sitting on was smashed. One of the tall apple trees had literally fallen over, the roots leaving a deep hole in the ground. Another tree had fallen on to one of the arks, smashing it completely. Again there were no tragedies apart from a huge dead rat obviously in the wrong place at the wrong time. There were always rats around the farm but their numbers were kept in check by the cats, owls and, of course, Rex.

The tree that had provided the nest site for the nuthatch had succumbed to the force of the wind. The crevice where the nest had been had given way and had split right down to the ground, one side falling away, narrowly missing another ark. I found the remains of the nest. Several trees had split boughs and there were twigs and small branches lying everywhere. The willow that overhung the orchard pond had lost a big bough that had fallen across the pond, forming a bridge. Grandad pointed out the remains of the wasps' nest that had obviously been supported by the bough and which now hung precariously from the trunk. Within a few days it had fallen into the water and Grandad fished it out for me. I spent hours dissecting the labyrinth of chambers and passageways.

The Nissen hut had survived the battering but the big willow at one end had not. It had been exposed to the full force of the gale and had lost two big limbs, one of which had split the trunk. The canal lock had not come out unscathed either. The big oak tree by the lock had lost one of its huge lower boughs, which had fallen partially into the canal, the other end still connected to the tree. The chainsaw was very busy for a long time afterwards removing split and damaged boughs and logging fallen trees. We had plenty of firewood after that; it's an ill wind!

Each of the seasons held a fascination for me. Winter brought its snow and frost. Spring heralded the period of renewal and new life, blossom in the orchard and all nature busily reproducing. Summer had long hot days and light nights, animals and birds raising their young, insects pollinating flowers; all aspects of nature rushing at full speed to complete the cycle. Autumn was the time of feeding up the summer migrants in preparation for their long flights to warmer climates; animals such as hedgehogs and dormice for their long hibernation. Many of our own resident birds feeding up to lay down fat reserves for the long winter ahead, the first frosts of late autumn killing off most of the remaining airborne insects. Finally, back to winter when nature sleeps.

The railway embankment was another source of wonder to

me during the spring, summer and autumn. I spent many days and hours up there throughout the year, watching and observing the wildlife of the seasons. By just sitting and being watchful one can learn a lot, whatever environment one is in.

From the base of the embankment to the track measured as high as seventy feet in places and this was a veritable nature reserve. Rex and I would spend many hours just sitting there watching the nature around us. It was bliss. Rex had incredible patience and would sit down when I did, more often than not falling asleep after a while.

Spring saw the cowslips, ragged robin, violets and speedwell flowering on the slopes. At the base in the more sheltered spots, arum lilies (lords and ladies) would flower. It was also time for the arrival of the first summer visitors such as willow warblers and chiffchaff to the embankment. They would fly between the scrubby bushes of blackthorn and hawthorn seeking out the early insects and singing at the same time. Rabbits were everywhere on the embankment and the spring brought the emergence of the first of the year's litters to the surface. By sitting perfectly still one could watch them quite closely.

As spring slipped into summer, the embankment became a blaze of colour as the yellow bird's-foot trefoil, the tall tufted vetch, clovers in red and white, poppy, scabious and large patches of the tall willow herb adorned it. Lizards could be seen basking in the summer sun. Some birds even nested on the embankment, notably the skylarks which hid their nests in the undergrowth, and a pair of spotted flycatchers which nested in one of the bushes. It was a precarious existence for all of the wildlife with the constant threat of fire during the summer months.

Early autumn saw a brilliant show of yellow as the poisonous ragwort came into flower. In some years this would take over stretches of the embankment completely. A close look at these plants would often reveal a small black and yellow caterpillar of the cinnebar moth. I later learned that these insects are quite remarkable. The caterpillars are able to store up the poison in their bodies, and their black and yellow markings warn other predators of their poisonous nature. Even more impressive is the fact that when the caterpillar pupates and eventually emerges as a handsome purple and black moth, it continues to carry the poison.

Other insects on the embankment included grass-hoppers, ants that provided food for the lizards and numerous butterflies: tortoiseshell, comma, blue, holly blue, painted lady, peacock and red admiral. The last two along with the brimstone could often be seen feeding on the flowering teasels that thrived here. Dragonflies would hunt along the slopes for flies and other airborne insects including the beautiful butterflies. The trains that rumbled past overhead and the plumes of smoke that enveloped the embankment did not seem to disturb or affect the wildlife in any way.

Along the side of the embankment, by the bridge that went over the canal, there was a large wooden board that had lain there for some time and a pair of field voles had taken up residence underneath. They would scuttle away when I lifted the board up but would soon return. They had built a beautiful ball-shaped nest of grass and I found eight naked tiny babies inside on one occasion. I carefully replaced the board and within a very short time I saw one of the adults return. I was thrilled to have seen the babies and even more excited to have seen an adult return. Months later when I visited, one vole scuttled away and the nest was otherwise empty.

Black ants were common on the embankment – their dome-like nests were dotted everywhere. Interestingly, there were no red ants. I used to sit and watch them for hours at a time. I was fascinated with their industriousness. Each individual appeared to have a specific role within the colony and on hot muggy days, as if by some common cue, the nests would erupt. Hundreds if not thousands of winged ants would emerge and fly off. These were larger and fatter than the rest of the colony, twice as big in many cases. Some struggled to get airborne and only managed to fly a short distance before crash landing; however, many rose high into the sky only to fall prey to swallows, house martins, flycatchers, starlings and even seagulls, which would join in the food bonanza. I later learned that these winged ants were pregnant females that flew off to establish another colony. Soon after landing, if they had survived the flight, they would shed their wings and bury into the soil to lay their eggs. Green woodpeckers were frequent visitors to the ant domes that they would attack with their sharp, powerful beaks. As the furious ants came to the surface, the bird would scoop them up with its long sticky tongue. It was fascinating to watch.

I recall one occasion when Rex and I were walking along the embankment in late June. It was a hot still day and I became aware of a low humming sound coming from the direction of the railway line above us. It seemed to be getting louder and louder when suddenly a black cloud came over the track about twenty-five yards behind us and descended the slope. It was a huge swarm of bees. I froze, terrified, mindful of what had happened to Corinne. Fortunately, the swarm struck and settled on a blackthorn sapling about level with us. I crouched down and watched. The bees had formed a massive ball of at least two feet in diameter. The bush was swaying with the weight of the swarm. The smoke from the trains rolling past above the swarm did not seem to affect it. Occasionally individuals would leave the ball, fly around it and then return as if on patrol. Sometimes there was a wave-type movement that swept around the ball. There was no breeze, so it could not have been that. I wondered if it was some form of synchronised movement by the bees on the outside to get further into the swarm, but later learned that it was probably a type of fanning system to cool the swarm. These wave movements did in fact increase as the afternoon wore on. As suddenly as it had arrived, the swarm moved off down the embankment, over the field next to the lane where the sheep were and into the orchard out of sight. I ran home with Rex to tell Grandad what I had seen and he was pleased. The bees were good for the orchard.

So there it was. My early years on the farm, with all its varied environments were a great influence on my developing natural history interests. My very close relationship with my grandfather, who would often take the time to explain things to me in a way that a youngster could understand, was also a great encouragement. It was Grandad who bought me my first set of Observer books that I read as much as I could from cover to cover. My mother and grandparents allowed me a lot of freedom at a very early age and this gave me the opportunity to look and listen with my old pal Rex. He was actually my uncle's dog but would spend most of his time with me, sitting happily by my side for many hours. I sometimes wonder what must have been going through his mind – if only dogs could speak. In many ways it was an idyllic world for a child to be brought up in the post-war years.

Sadly, in 1959 this was all to come to an abrupt end. In the early spring of that year, a deadly disease of poultry struck the farm, known as fowl pest. This was a notifiable disease to the police and ultimately the Ministry. Within a day there was a sign on the farm gate stating, 'RESTRICTED ACCESS. MINISTRY CONTROLLED AREA. BY ORDER OF HM GOVERNMENT.' Over the course of the next few days, Ministry officials destroyed all the poultry. Fowl pest is a fatal disease affecting the birds' eyes and respiratory tracts; death follows shortly afterwards. At ten years old I could not understand what was happening and the speed with which everything was carried out. All the dead poultry were burned on a huge fire by the side of the orchard pond, along with all the arks and hen houses in the orchard. The bedding and perches in the Nissen hut were ripped out and burned and the inside of the hut was soaked in a chemical before being sealed by Ministry padlocks.

Grandad helped the Ministry officials as best he could but it must have devastated him to see everything that he had built up, literally destroyed overnight. I was not allowed into the orchard or over to Seabrook. I had to walk to school in wellington boots having stood in a bath of chemicals at the gate as I left and again on my return. I had to put my shoes on at school and wellington boots back on for the return walk to the farm.

The farm remained sealed off for over three months and it fell very quiet in the orchard and all around. I could not understand why Grandad had not restocked with poultry but he was spending a lot of time away from the farm. Unbeknown to me, he was making arrangements to sell the farm, as the Ministry would not allow him to restock with any livestock for five years. Within a short space of time a buyer from Pitstone was found and after the autumn fruit harvest the farm was sold.

It was a very sad day when our removal van arrived. Mum, Corinne and I moved to Ivinghoe about two miles away, immediately in the shadow of Ivinghoe Beacon, one of the tallest of the Chilterns. My uncle Andrew placed Rex in a kennel at Leighton Buzzard whilst he sorted a few things out. Tragically, I never saw Rex again after a tearful goodbye behind the removal lorry, as he escaped from the kennel and was never seen again.

The next few years of my life were turbulent ones. We did not stay in Ivinghoe for long. My mother remarried and we moved to West London, which I found very claustrophobic after the freedom of the farm and open countryside. Then the opportunity of a lifetime came my way.

Top: Narrow boat moored.
Bottom: Swing bridge and railway embankment.

Top: Threshing machine and tractor.
Bottom: Lock gates with Seabrook to the right.

Top: Wren.
Bottom: Claudius and Claudette the Brazilian Tapiers (Claudius licking his lips).

Top: Twirpy.
Bottom: Guillemots.

Top: N' Pongo.
Bottom: Common Buzzard.

Top: Cormorant.
Bottom: Brown five-inch dragonfly.

Top: The author and Dave Kinnley.
Bottom: Fallow deer doe.

Top: North American ferruginous hawk 'Gorbash'.
Bottom: A pair of barn owls.

Jersey Zoo

The Jersey Zoo was formed in March 1959 by the author and naturalist Gerald Durrell at Augres Manor, Trinity, Jersey. Its purpose was to breed endangered species of animals and birds and eventually to return their offspring to the wild. To finance the establishment of the zoo and the initial collecting trips all over the world but in particular South America, Gerald Durrell used money from his early books such as the *Bafut Beagles* and *My Family and Other Animals*, both of which became best-sellers in the 1950s. In 1963 the zoo became the Jersey Wildlife Preservation Trust with a board of trustees but Durrell continued to support the trust for many years.

To quote Durrell, 'The world is as delicate and as complicated as a spider's web. If you touch one thread you send shudders running through all the other threads. We are not just touching the web; we are tearing great holes in it. The trusts I have created are dedicated to preserving some of the casualties. Each mammal, bird or reptile with which we are concerned has taken millions of years to evolve. Suddenly it is in peril of its life and if we do not act very quickly will be lost from the face of the earth for ever.' I believe that this quote sums up the work of the zoo very eloquently.

It was early December 1964, just after my fifteenth birthday, that a letter that was to change my life dropped through the door. It was from Jersey Zoo inviting me to the island for an interview for a keeper's job. I could not believe my luck. I had written to the zoo at my mother's suggestion, as Durrell, along with Attenborough, was one of my heroes. I had read all of his books and avidly watched his programmes on the television. I was now being given the remote chance of working with him at his zoo.

The interview was in early January 1965 and I could hardly contain my excitement. I nervously boarded the British Rail ferry *Sarnia* at Weymouth; I wanted this job badly. It was a nine-hour crossing through a gale and it was very rough. Eventually, we docked at St Helier and I took my first steps on the island that was to become my adopted home. I was greeted by one of the keepers, John McGregor, in a beaten up old Mini. He talked constantly for the entire journey and by the time we had left St Helier I knew his life story. He was twenty-five, an ex-marine and he had been working at the zoo for two years. As we reached the zoo I knew everything I needed to know about it as well as much about Gerald and Jacquie Durrell.

The car park was of loose gravel and full of quite large potholes. John parked the car next to an open lean-to that was full of sawdust and shavings – this was the bedding store. We walked down the slope passing a paddock with tapirs, another with peccaries and further down enclosures with mandrills, gelada baboons and the last enclosure housed a beautiful spectacled bear, one of John's charges. As we entered the house, I was a little nervous to say the least. John left me with a lady in the office and, as he left, he wished me good luck. The lady was one of the secretaries, Betty Bouzard, and she led me into a large room with books lining three of the four walls from floor to ceiling. A picture window overlooked the large lawn and ornamental garden. I believe that Betty sensed my nervousness, so she brought me a cup of tea.

I sat admiring the books, which I later learned were part of Durrell's collection, when suddenly the door opened and in walked a tall man with blond hair who was very well spoken. He introduced himself as the zoo director, Jeremy

Mallinson. He immediately put me at ease by cracking jokes about the rough crossing. We sat and talked for over an hour. I told him about the farm and he told me of the zoo and its aims. He was quite impressed with my knowledge of Durrell and the zoo; I had done my homework well. We then had a guided tour. Starting in the large ape house, I was introduced to the gorillas, Nandy and N'Pongo, the male chimpanzee, Chumley, and his females, Sheena and Be Be, along with the two orang-utans, Oscar and Bali. I also met Dingle the chough and Sidney the herring gull which could not fly and which patrolled the zoo pecking at the odd visitor.

On the slope that I had walked down with John, I met the spectacled bear, Pedro, the male mandrill, Frisky, the Brazilian tapirs, the male called Claudius and the female called Claudette with their baby, Juno. The peccaries were running round their paddock, this being normal behaviour for them according to Jeremy. I met the two leopards, Lokai the male and Gerda the female. The New Guinea singing dogs were very attractive and had a litter of pups. In the small mammal house I came across Celebes monkeys, marmosets, ring-tailed lemurs, one of which was called Polly, tenrecs, fennec foxes, spiny anteaters, tree shrews and various monkeys. Back outside we walked past numerous aviaries with birds of prey including bateleur eagles and owls such as the snowy, European eagle and the spectacled owl. On the walk down to an area that Jeremy had referred to as 'The Swannery' we passed further aviaries containing parrots of varying descriptions and macaws including a beautiful blue macaw called Mr Coe. The swannery was a natural wet area with ponds, streams and lots of mud. It was full of wildfowl: tree ducks, wood ducks, mandarin, swans and various geese.

Another path led us past a huge enclosure full of very noisy colobus monkeys, their long black and white coats and lengthy white tails blowing in the strong breeze, the remains of the previous night's gale. Jeremy filled me in on the

45

breeding record, character and sometimes regaled me with amusing anecdotes on each of the individuals that we met. At the staff quarters he left me with John. He asked me to return to the office later as he was going to discuss my possible employment with Catha Weller, the company secretary. John led me into a large kitchen, which I soon learned was the main meeting area for all the keepers. I had a cup of tea and chatted with him as various staff members came and went. It was a hive of activity.

I later returned to the office where I rejoined Jeremy. With a smile on his face he said that I had been successful and asked when I could start. I replied, 'Straight away.' He then led me into another room where I met Jacquie Durrell, who was quite charming and she welcomed me into the fold. We chatted for quite a while and she apologised that Gerald was not there but he was abroad on a collecting trip. We sat and had a further cup of tea before she bid me a safe journey home, saying that she looked forward to my joining the team at the zoo. I went back to the office where some administration details were completed, said goodbye to everyone and then John took me back to St Helier for the 6 p.m. ferry home.

I remember standing on the deck leaning on the rail and looking out to sea, thinking how lucky I was and pondering over everything that had happened over the past few hours. There was a strong breeze in my face as I thought about the future. I remained up on deck for most of the trip back to Weymouth. I was too excited to sleep despite being very tired as I had had little sleep on the crossing over. It was still dark when we landed at Weymouth but I managed to find a phone box and rang Mum to tell her the news. I had forgotten that it was 4.30 a.m. and she was not amused but deep down she was pleased for me.

I was due to start at the zoo in three weeks' time and I had a lot to sort out; it was a rather frantic time. Eventually, the day arrived and I said my goodbyes at home before making my way back to Weymouth with two suitcases and boarding the ferry for the crossing to a new and exciting chapter in my life.

This time, Phil Coffey, the ape keeper, whom I had met briefly on my initial visit, met me at St Helier. John McGregor greeted us at the zoo car park in a small tractor/trailer contraption. Phil and I climbed on board with my suitcases and we roared down the slope coming to an abrupt halt at the staff kitchen. John gave me a beaming smile as I picked myself up off the floor of the trailer. Phil took me to my room, which overlooked an enclosure of lions and had views of some of the other big cats. It was a small simple room with a bed along one wall, a tiny table on another and a compact wardrobe in one corner. It was very snug. John brought me a cup of tea as I unpacked and generally settled in. The room next to mine belonged to John 'Shep' Mallett, and at the end of the corridor another room was home to Jill Watson. John was the curator of birds, and Jill of reptiles. At the evening meal I was introduced to some of the other members of staff including Martin Carslake, Quentin Bloxham, George Jacobs, Stefan Ormorod, Jill Watson and Malcolm Noyes. I was given a meal and it soon became apparent that everyone mucked in together. Jeremy called in and welcomed me to the family. I was the newest and youngest member of staff and I was taken under Shep's wing, so to speak.

The first few days were a period of settling in and learning the ropes. Work started at 7 a.m. every day. My first responsibility was the tropical bird house where we had mynahs, mousebirds, touracos, and a pair of red-thighed falconettes and finches of all descriptions. The house had a central walkway for visitors with large aviaries running down each side and along the bottom. The temperature was a constant 75°F and the humidity was very high, so one soon worked up a sweat in there. The touracos' aviary had a glass front on the inside section but they had a large outdoor section as well, as these birds are fruit eaters and quite messy, similar to the mynahs. The peat floors of all the aviaries in the house were raked over and generally freshened up. The peat in each was replaced once a week on a rotational basis, resulting in one aviary having fresh peat each day. The back walls and wire frontages were washed every day and the mynahs and touracos took first prize for being the messiest.

Once all the cleaning had been completed, food was put out and the floor area where the public walked was washed down, this being the final job. The zoo opened to the public at 10 a.m. and all the general work had to be completed by that time. After breakfast the remainder of the day was spent helping one another out. The tasks included building new enclosures, renewing undergrowth in established enclosures, treating ill or injured animals and birds and caring for residents of the quarantine section in the roof of a barn that housed the baboons and mandrills. One was never bored and there was no time to walk around the zoo with your hands in your pockets.

It was not long after I started at the zoo that the first of many amusing incidents occurred. Pedro, the spectacled bear, had a reputation for escaping and one day he did just that. I was helping Jill in the reptile house, another hot and humid area, when the door flew open and someone shouted that Pedro had escaped. He had apparently run up the slope, across the car park and into the field on the opposite side of the lane. I ran over to the field with a group of keepers and there was Pedro, halfway up a wooden pylon gazing around at the scenery. There was a great deal of deliberation about how to get him down without injury. A drug dart would be effective but the fear was that as the drug took effect he would fall and injure himself – which nobody wanted. The staff who had initially given chase had managed to lasso him around his neck but he had simply dragged them across the field, as he was an incredibly powerful animal. They had subsequently been forced to let go when he had climbed the pole and the rope still dangled down, bearing testimony to their efforts.

There was a great fear that he might continue to climb the pole to the high voltage cables at the top and we were in a real dilemma. How could we attempt to get Pedro down without injuring himself? How could we prevent him from going to the top of the pole and frying himself, not to mention knocking out the power to the zoo? Everybody was trying to call him down but he was just ignoring us and the language of the keepers was becoming quite blue. Suddenly, without warning Pedro let go of the pole and dropped like a stone landing squarely on two keepers, one of whom was Quentin. They stood up, looking dazed but uninjured. Pedro was standing on his hind legs and at well over six feet was very impressive, but there was not an ounce of aggression in him.

Shep then remembered an idea that had apparently worked the last time that Pedro had escaped. He ran back to the zoo and returned shortly with a box of Smarties. Pedro was sitting quite happily on the ground with a circle of keepers around him. A Smartie was thrown to him and he caught it in his mouth. The sweet taste obviously registered with him immediately, for he stood up and beckoned for more. A couple of sweets were thrown on to the ground and he nosed around and found them. A thin trail was then laid with the Smarties and Pedro was happy to follow; as far as he was concerned this was a good game. The trail led back to the zoo, through the car park and down the slope to his enclosure. We all followed at a discreet distance with our fingers crossed. On reaching his enclosure, the remainder of the sweets were tipped on to the floor just inside the door, and without any hesitation Pedro walked in and the door was shut. He took no notice of us; he was more interested in the chocolates. Luckily, the rifle with the tranquilliser dart remained locked away in the office on this occasion. The weapon was capable of firing either a dart, or a solid round – the final solution.

The first of many injuries I sustained came shortly after the Pedro incident. In the tropical bird house we had a common mynah called Tuppence. She was a small bird, slate grey in colour with a bright yellow eye flash. She lived in an aviary on her own but with rosy starling next to her for company. Tuppence was renowned for her ability to recite poetry; she was very eloquent and was a popular bird with the visitors. She was extremely tame and when I was working in the house on my own she would come out and sit on my head as I went about my tasks. On this particular occasion I had nearly finished washing the floor of the house and Tuppence was happily sitting in her usual spot in the middle of my head, when suddenly she flew off. This was unusual in itself. She flew to the other end of the house, turned around in a sharp circle in front of the touracos and then back towards me. I naturally thought that she was going to land back on my head, but at the very last moment of her approach, I realised she was going for my face. I ducked and she flew over my head making a squawking noise that I had not heard before. She had obviously turned at an acute angle because as I stood up and looked round to see what she was up to she caught me full face and pecked me hard above my left eye. She appeared to be trying to peck my eyes out. My instant reaction was to brush her away but she pressed home the attack and caught me in the same place again. This time I managed to grab her and I put her back in her aviary. The names I called her are unrepeatable and certainly were not Tuppence.

As I had blood streaming down my face, I went to the

kitchen to clean it up. As is so typical of head wounds, the copious amounts of blood that were shed seemed somewhat excessive for the small cut which was revealed after cleaning. A plaster covered the wound nicely. Shep could not believe what had happened, especially when we went back into the bird house to see the miscreant sitting on her perch looking as innocent as ever. Shep let her out and she landed on his head and just looked at me. She then flew on to my head and sang 'Ring a Ring a Roses' and we both burst out laughing.

We never did discover what had caused this aggressive behaviour. Shep's theory was that maybe one of the other birds in the house had spooked her, but we shall never know. The general comment in the staff kitchen was that she didn't like the way I had looked at her! I always treated her with the utmost respect when I let her out after that and she never attacked me again. However, this was only the first of many injuries I was to sustain during my time at the zoo, when I discovered that not all animals and birds are friendly.

Sidney, the herring gull, soon latched on to me and would follow me around everywhere. His inability to fly did not slow him up very much; he could run around incredibly fast and had no difficulty in keeping up with me even when I was in my usual hurry. I would feed him the odd titbit from the kitchen but he did very well from the visitors, particularly in the summer when they would sit outside the restaurant, which in those days was part of the main house, and eat their food. He was a very persistent scrounger.

My first visit to the casualty department in the hospital at St Helier was courtesy of one of Sidney's cousins. It was early one morning, the zoo had just opened and I was in the kitchen when I was despatched to the entrance kiosk to collect an injured seabird. On my arrival I found a young girl holding a lesser black-backed gull that was wrapped in a towel. She told me that she and her mother had found the bird on the beach at Bouley Bay and that it had apparently broken a wing. I took the bird in the towel and started to walk down the slope. These gulls are large birds with bright yellow eyes. Its head was clear of the towel and it started to struggle, so I held it to my chest and it appeared to settle. Suddenly and without any warning, the bird reached up and pecked me on the inside of my nose. Its beak was either side of the nasal septum that separates the nostrils and had gone up quite a way. My immediate reaction was to pull the bird away but, as I did so, the hook on the top beak ripped into the septum and blood gushed out, initially all over the bird. The pain was excruciating and my eyes were watering uncontrollably. I reached the bottom of the slope and Martin Carslake, who was walking past, helped me to the kitchen and took the bird. We could not stop the bleeding, so with ice packs on my nose and a towel I was taken to the hospital. After examination, the treatment was continued – ice packs and an antiseptic cream. My nose took a long time to recover, which was more than could be said for the gull. Its wing was broken right at the top near the breast and it had to be put down humanely.

There was another character, apart from Sidney, that I grew very fond of. He was Dingle the chough which lived in a huge aviary near the ape house. He would run along the edge of the aviary as you passed and if you stopped he would brush his head backwards along the mesh, thereby roughing up his feathers. He would enjoy nothing more than having the back of his head stroked, when his beautiful bright red curled beak would sway backwards and forwards in pleasure. As a special treat, I would feed him a mealworm, not of course forgetting Sidney who would always be nearby.

One bird that arrived at the zoo was to present us with a fairly unique problem. A little old lady who was no longer able to give her the vast amount of attention she required presented an Indian mynah bird called Asia to the zoo. Asia was a fine specimen with a lovely sheen to her black feathers and a bright yellow eye flash. Shep decided that she should join the five other mynahs which were in an aviary in the bird house, so in she went and was accepted straight away. Despite this, we did keep a close watch on them for a few days but all seemed to be well. She settled in quickly and even started jumping on to my shoulder when I was in the aviary cleaning the back wall and mesh front.

One morning the routine was as normal. I climbed into the mynah's aviary and set about scrubbing the back wall. Asia was sitting on a perch with the other birds. Suddenly, I heard the words 'F— off' as clear as a bell. I looked around in amazement expecting to see one of my colleagues standing nearby but there was nobody there. I stepped out of the aviary and looked outside but there was no sign of anyone there either. Then, there it was again, 'F— off', as clear as anything. I glanced around thinking that someone was playing a joke on me but I was on my own. I finished cleaning the house and at breakfast time I told Shep. His comment was, 'You should take more water with it next time.' The following day it happened again and I began to suspect that it was one of the mynahs. The third day I gained Shep's assistance to watch the birds and this confirmed my suspicion that it was Asia that was swearing. Shep found it very amusing but there was a serious side to it, as we could not risk having Asia swearing at the visitors. The problem was brought to Jeremy's attention and the decision made that Asia should be moved to the quarantine section in the interest of public 'safety'. She joined another mynah there that had plucked out all its breast feathers and looked quite unsightly but was otherwise in good health. I should point out that Asia did not pick up her bad language from me despite the thoughts of one or two of the other keepers.

The quarantine section in those early days also doubled as a hospital and it was to prove to be very useful when the Torre Canyon oil tanker sank off the coast of Cornwall, spewing thousands of gallons of crude oil into the sea. As the huge oil slick broke up, some of it affected the Channel Isles. It was the first major oil disaster in Britain and was an environmental calamity. We had a lot of seabirds brought in to us, the majority of which were too pathetic to save. Most of these birds were guillemots and we were able to rescue about six. We had to force feed them to begin with, giving them slivers of fish, which was no mean feat, but as they settled in and built up their strength they started to feed themselves. Once they were more or less fully fit we took them up to Le Tacq, a rocky outcrop at the western end of the island and released them. It was lovely to watch them fly off the rocks and settle on the water, diving and bathing, happy to be free again. We watched them for some time, as the sun set across the water and it was one of those magical moments. As we drove back to the zoo, I felt really pleased with myself, although of course it had been a team effort.

Another bird that came in at about the same time as Asia was a ringed plover. Its wing was not broken but the tip of it had twisted right around and therefore the bird could not fly. The next time the vet visited, he examined the bird but the prognosis was not good. Basically, there was nothing he could do for it. The bird itself was otherwise healthy and feeding quite happily. Shep decided that it would be cruel to release it into the wild, as a predator would take it, so it would live in the bird house. The decision was made to put it in the mousebird aviary, as they would not pose a threat to it. They are fruit eaters and never come down on to the floor of the aviary, so the bird soon settled into its new home. I fed it on insects, mainly mealworms, which it loved, and the plover became a popular character with the visitors. We placed a small plaque on the outside of the aviary with a brief résumé of how the bird came to be there.

It was a good two months after I had started work at the zoo before I met Gerald Durrell himself. He had been on a collecting trip to Sierra Leone and had brought back some lovely exotic birds that were temporarily housed in the quarantine section – more company for Asia. One morning just after breakfast, Jacquie came into the kitchen as she often did and said that Gerry wanted to see me. I was a little nervous as I held him in great awe and I said I would change, but Jacquie said not to bother, so I followed her into the house in my wellington boots and dirty jeans. We went into the room with the floor to ceiling books and there he was. We shook hands and he beckoned me to sit. I told him that my jeans were dirty but he dismissed that with a wave of his hand before Jacquie left us to it. He offered me a cup of coffee, jokingly saying that it was a bit early for anything stronger and I was soon put at my ease.

He asked me about myself and whether I was enjoying working at the zoo; my reply made him chuckle. He had a wonderful sense of humour which became more and more apparent as we talked. He spoke of his aims for the future and the trips that he was planning and I was totally absorbed. Here I was talking quite freely with one of my childhood heroes; it was a wonderful moment. We sat and talked for over an hour and a half and a further cup of coffee was brought in. Towards the end of our chat Gerry said something that I will never forget. He was talking about the future of the zoo and said, 'Of course I long to see the day when I can close the zoo, as it would no longer be needed,' but he knew that day would never come. Eventually the telephone rang and he had someone to see him. He was a busy man, but as I left he said that we must talk again, and we did, many times.

Soon after this meeting, a problem arose with the male orang-utan, Oscar. He had found a way of removing the strips of wood in the roof of the outside section of his enclosure. The roof comprised wooden slats similar to parquet flooring and Oscar had somehow managed to get his fingernail between the joints, which I would have thought was impossible. He had already removed three slats before a visitor brought it to our attention. With some difficulty we managed to get a very reluctant Oscar into his inside quarters and shut him in. The damage was assessed and it was decided to place sheets of steel over the complete ceiling. I remember the look that Jeremy gave Oscar when he came to examine the damage, but Oscar simply stared back with utter contempt.

With the repairs completed, Oscar and Bali were allowed out into the outer section with the new steel ceiling. Oscar wasted no time in examining the repairs. We had moved the beams around to reduce his access to the ceiling but this had little effect as he simply climbed the bars to look at it. He was not a happy chap but we had won that battle, or had we? A few days later Phil had watched Oscar who had been spending all his time at the ceiling. Using his fingernail again, he had managed to unscrew a couple of the retaining screws that the contractors had used to secure the steel sheets. Once again he was shut in while the contractors came back and painstakingly bevelled all the screws flush, removing the groove in the head to prevent Oscar getting a purchase with his nail. With some trepidation Oscar was allowed back out and again he went straight to the ceiling. This time, however, we had won, much to Oscar's frustration.

Another confrontation involving Oscar was quite amusing. It revolved around four ceramic tiles that Jersey Pottery had made showing a picture of Oscar, with his name underneath. The tiles were fixed to the wall outside the outer section of the orang-utan's enclosure. For some reason Oscar took an instant dislike to the tiles and immediately tried to prise them off with his nail. They were removed out of his reach and all was well for about six months. Then, one evening Phil was giving Oscar his medicine with a long-handled metal spoon. Suddenly, Oscar grabbed the spoon out of Phil's hand and immediately and very deliberately ran outside. Phil shouted to me for assistance, as I happened to be in the ape house kitchen at the time. I went outside to see what Oscar was up to this time and found him trying to prise the tiles off with the spoon. Fortunately, I had arrived in time. We took the tiles down and placed them behind the glass in the inside quarters, out of Oscar's reach. It was quite uncanny, as though Oscar had planned what he was going to do with the spoon even before he stole it. With his arm at full stretch through the outside bars, the spoon had given him not only the ability to reach the tiles but also the rigidity to prise them off. It was a long time before the spoon was retrieved, as Oscar would carry it around with him all the time.

Oscar and I had a face-to-face confrontation one day, which could easily have ended with a serious injury to myself and it would have been my own fault for lack of concentration. It was autumn time and I had been detailed to sweep up the leaves that had collected against the outside quarters of the ape house in the six-foot gap between the public barrier and the house itself. I was busily sweeping away and was aware that Oscar's eyes were fixed on me from deep within his enclosure. I was wearing one of the new zoo issue woollen jumpers, which were coloured mottled green, black and white. I had, in fact, borrowed Quentin's, as my own was in the wash. As I swept the leaves in front of Oscar, he moved up to the bars and watched me intently with those piercing eyes. I was concentrating more on the broom than myself as I thought that he might make a lunge for it.

Suddenly, his foot shot through the bars and grabbed my

jumper firmly. I put the broom down quite calmly over the barrier and turned to face him; we were eye to eye. I tried to break his grip but almost immediately his other foot came through and grabbed another part of the jumper. His eyes were fixed on me and not once did he look down to see what his feet were doing. I tried to pull away but his powerful grip held firm and the jumper simply stretched. I tried talking to him but my words fell upon deaf ears. Without warning he pulled with his feet so quickly that I found myself up against the bars and, before I had time to react, his arms came through and grabbed the jumper in the region of my chest. Now I was pinned up against the bars and with nobody around to help me. Oscar was still staring at me and had not averted his glare once.

I could feel the pressure slowly increasing as he started to pull the jumper. This was potentially a dangerous situation for me as Oscar had the strength to cause me a serious injury. In a flash I had taken the jumper off and broken away from him. He immediately pulled the jumper through the bars and ran off to the inside quarters. Quite badly shaken, I leapt the barrier, grabbed the broom and ran around to see what Oscar was doing. He was proudly displaying his prize. He had tried to put the jumper on but had only managed to get his feet through the arms and the bottom of the jumper was around his waist; it looked like a giant nappy. I fetched Phil who thought it was highly amusing, although I was more concerned about telling Quentin what had happened to his jumper. Needless to say, he did not find it funny. The office replaced the jumper for him and I received a roasting from Jeremy because all of the apes should have been shut in before work started in clearing the leaves. I had learned my lesson the hard way.

Oscar was quite a character and I was very fond of him despite his devious nature. By total contrast, Bali was quiet and placid and would come out and have a walk round on her hind legs. It was during one of these walkabouts when Oscar was shut out that the remains of the jumper were recovered in shreds. Quentin suggested that I use the wool to knit a new one.

Another trip to hospital was the result of assisting Malcolm Noyes in the small mammal house. I had finished my tasks and he asked me if I could give him a hand after breakfast, as he wanted to clean out and revamp the ring-tailed lemur enclosure. The small mammal house was of similar design to the bird house, with a central pathway for visitors and enclosures on either side and across the bottom end. The kitchen was at the other end where all the various feeds were prepared. I had been in with the lemurs on many occasions when helping Malcolm, and I grabbed a broom to sweep up the sawdust on the floor. There were four lemurs in this enclosure including the most extrovert of the group, Polly. She would regularly sit on the shoulder of anyone that happened to be in there; the rest were a little timid.

I took some chopped banana in as a treat for them all; Malcolm was outside preparing some new branches that were going in their enclosure. Polly and the others ate the banana and, as I swept away humming to myself, Polly jumped on to my shoulder then on to my head where she started grooming my hair. There should have been no live inhabitants in my hair, which was virtually in a crew cut, but she still had to search, as this type of grooming is a bonding instinct. As I swept the floor, I tried to keep my head as still as possible for her and I could feel her long black and white tail down my back. Suddenly I spotted a drop of fresh blood on the floor and then another. I instinctively looked up thinking that Polly had been injured somehow, and she promptly jumped off my head on to a nearby perch. As I looked at her, blood started to pour down my face and the cold realisation came over me that it was mine.

At that moment Malcolm came in and looked at me in horror, shouting some unrepeatable expletive. He rushed over and helped me out of the enclosure. Neither of us could work out what had happened initially but it soon became apparent that Polly had opened my head up with the razor-type bite that lemurs are renowned for. I was assisted to the staff kitchen where my head was wrapped in a towel and once again I was taken to the casualty department of the hospital. I had sustained a four-inch cut to the top right side of my head, which had to be shaved before they could sew it up. It took fifty stitches to bind the wound together and I had to have two days off work. By now you may be thinking that I am accident-prone but, although everyone sustained the odd injury, I only remember mine. Gerry was in the process of preparing for a major trip to Argentina but he took time out to see me; I looked quite impressive with a turban-type bandage around my head. He was genuinely concerned and nobody could understand what made Polly act the way she did. Whilst still wearing the head bandage, I went to see her but she was totally uninterested!

We had six pairs of cape barren geese (cereopsis) that are a particularly rare type of goose that we had been trying to breed for some time. They were pinioned and therefore could not fly, and although they had free range of the zoo, most of their time was spent in or near the swannery. They were slate grey with an almost luminescent green beak. Shep and I had discussed whether the lack of breeding might have been due to competition from other geese in particular the Canada geese, which were very aggressive and territorial. We decided to approach Jeremy with a view to placing the cape barrens in an empty enclosure near to the zoo entrance, which was eventually to house silver and white-eared pheasants. This would establish whether confinement and the avoidance of any competition would encourage them to breed. Jeremy agreed, but our time was restricted to one season only.

The enclosure was a large one with plenty of cover at one end and a large bed of stinging nettles. It was next to the enclosure containing bennetts wallabies for which Gerry and Jeremy were anxious to establish a breeding colony along with the two breeds of pheasants previously mentioned. There was a little element of competitiveness as London Zoo was also trying to breed them. I was seconded to dig and line a pond in the new enclosure and the geese were rounded up. This was no mean feat but they soon settled into their new shelter. The following spring brought success. The geese built two nests in the nettles and each pair hatched off four young.

It was cause for celebration and Gerry was delighted. I was especially pleased to have been a part of it. I sat with Shep in his room one night talking of the problem that we now faced – moving the geese out in favour of the pheasants. We discussed it late into the night. Shep had two monkeys in a huge cage that filled one wall in his bedroom and an African grey parrot that was loose. They all joined in the conversation. We decided that Shep would suggest to Jeremy that we place the pheasants in with the geese for a trial period, as the enclosure was more than large enough. Jeremy agreed but, although the geese continued to breed, the pheasants did not and were eventually moved to their own enclosure on a bank overlooking the swannery.

In a more unusual part of my role at the zoo I was called as a prosecution witness to give evidence of identification of a curlew. It had been shot on the island and the States' Police were prosecuting the person responsible for shooting a protected species. The police had first approached Shep as curator of birds but he had suggested that I do it as it would be good experience for me – in reality he did not want to go to court himself. The police duly arrived one morning with a deep frozen curlew, which I had no difficulty in identifying. It had been preserved in this way as it was to be produced as evidence in court. The gentleman concerned was pleading not guilty and I had to make a formal statement to the police confirming that the bird they had shown me was a curlew and a protected species. I was subsequently summoned to attend court and confirm the identification. I was really nervous and cursing Shep. As it turned out the ordeal was not as bad as I had expected. The defendant pleaded guilty at the last moment but I was still asked to declare to the court that the bird was a curlew. I was in the witness box for about thirty seconds and it was a bit nerve-racking. A substantial one hundred pound fine was levied, which in those days was an awful lot of money.

I previously mentioned that when Polly tried to reshape my head Gerald Durrell was about to leave on a trip to Argentina. I will always remember his return. That night we held a staff party, as we did on a regular basis. This particular party was for George Jacobs who was leaving to drive over land in a Mini Moke to India, where he planned to write a book. Copious amounts of alcohol were drunk and at about 11 p.m. we were requested to go to the airport and collect a shipment of live birds that Durrell had collected. We leapt aboard the zoo truck and drove to the airport where the plane, a Dakota, was being unloaded. Once all the crates had cleared customs, we organised them in the truck and returned to the zoo; it was imperative that we got the new arrivals housed and settled in as quickly as possible. The various boxes were taken up to the quarantine section and the birds placed in their allotted aviaries.

The entire operation ran very smoothly, which was surprising really in view of the condition we were in. However, there had to be one awkward customer. One of the keepers accidentally released a pygmy owl that stood all of three inches high. It flew up on to one of the crossbeams that lined the roof of the barn above our heads. There then followed an absolutely hilarious few minutes, as attempts were made to try and catch this bird that seemed to be quite happy flying from beam to beam. If you can imagine a group of men slightly under the influence trying to catch a tiny bird with what I would describe as butterfly nets, you will understand how comical the situation was. I can only say that the bird's reactions were a lot quicker than ours. Everybody was looking upwards and not where he or she was going, so we were crashing into each other as well as into the upright posts supporting the barn. Fortunately, all the other cages were covered over, so the occupants were unaware of the cause of the mayhem outside. The language was blue. Eventually, someone managed to net the owl and it was placed in its cage with no apparent ill effects. If only I had had my camera then.

In due course, the new arrivals were housed in the bird house. I remember the emerald toucanettes, which were most attractive and were placed in with the mynahs. Being fruit eaters, this meant that the aviary had to be cleaned out twice daily. The pygmy owl joined some other owls near the otters.

After about two years on the bird section I was asked if I could increase my responsibilities to include the tapirs, peccaries and the pets' corner that had recently been completed. I agreed but it was acknowledged that the bird house would take priority in the morning. As it was there was not too much to do with these extra animals apart from feeding and general maintenance. They were only cleaned out occasionally and this could be done once the zoo had opened. There were ten South American peccaries that were breeding well. The piglets in their black and fawn spotted coats were quite attractive; however, the adults could be vicious. The dominant boar had huge tusks that I discovered on one occasion when he bit the toe of my wellington. Miraculously the two tusks passed between my toes. If they hadn't, at least one toe would have been severed. A strong stick accompanied me after that, although the following Christmas the old boar died; I still have his tusks somewhere.

The tapirs were a completely different kettle of fish. Claudius, the male, was very bad-tempered and unpredictable, whereas his female, Claudette, was quiet, friendly and good-natured. She suffered with a skin complaint similar to dermatitis, which we treated with regular baths, cream and Aureomycin spray that temporarily turned her skin purple. She loved the bath and all the attention. Their baby Juno was really sweet; a tiny speckled miniature of her parents. She spent a lot of her time in their hut, as she was shy of visitors. Tapirs are herbivores, feeding in the wild on swamp vegetation, and at the zoo they lived on a very healthy diet of fruit and vegetables, which they thrived on.

On one occasion I was in their paddock placing the food in their metal feeding trough at the far side. Claudette and Juno had followed me across as usual and Claudius had stayed back. I was just finishing emptying the second bucket into the trough when I heard a pounding-type noise and almost immediately someone shouted, 'Barry, behind you.' I glanced round to see Claudius charging at me with full speed. His trunk-like nose was in the air, showing his teeth quite clearly. I dropped the buckets and ran for the fence but, as I leapt over, Claudius grabbed my right buttock and bit hard. As I picked myself up off the driveway, I could feel a trickle running down my leg. Once again I had to visit the hospital for yet more stitches. Claudius had bitten so hard that he had pulled out some of the buttock muscle and I had to undergo minor surgery to repair the wound. The nurses thought it was hilarious with me lying there on my front and my backside exposed. I am sure they did not have to be quite so savage with the anaesthetic needle. Sitting was a problem for quite a while and I was the 'butt' of many jokes in the staff kitchen. Thankfully, this injury along with Polly's cut were the two most serious I was to sustain whilst working at the zoo.

It was about this time that there were great celebrations around the zoo as one of the female chimpanzees, Sheena, had given birth to a baby female named Alexa. But joy soon turned to real concern because Sheena had rejected her baby and there was fear for the infant's welfare. The decision was taken that Alexa should be removed from Sheena, and I will always remember seeing Alexa cowering in the corner as her mother ran around screaming and charging towards her. Time was of the essence and the problem was how to separate the two. Food is a wonderful distraction, however, even in highly charged situations such as this. Sheena had been segregated from the others, as it was feared that Chumley would kill the baby as soon as it was born. This meant we only had Sheena to contend with. As it turned out she was quite easily coaxed outside and the sliding door was closed behind her. She was not overly concerned and was more interested in the banana. Alexa was brought out and was immediately given some milk, as she had not suckled from her mother. Jill volunteered to look after her with help from all the staff. I was ideally placed to help as Jill and I shared the same landing. Shep already had his two monkeys and Polly, and of course his Alsatian bitch Reema as well as a miniature Schnauzer, so his room was full to overflowing.

Alexa was absolutely beautiful with her soft, soulful eyes, little round face and those huge ears that were almost as big as her face. She soon settled down with us. When she was with me she would sleep in a dog basket at the end of my bed and, as soon as my head appeared above the blankets, she would groom my hair and beard. This was bonding behaviour, although she preferred Jill's hair, which was longer than my crew cut. While she groomed, her lips were smacking. She was particularly fascinated in the scar left by Polly's bite, which had a lump at one end that she would pay special attention to but she never once hurt it. She was very gentle even as she grew, and I would reciprocate her grooming with the same lip-smacking sound, which she loved.

If I ever overslept and rushed out to work without being groomed, Alexa would throw a real temper tantrum and would be in a terrible mood for the rest of the day. I would check on her from time to time and if she was in one of her moods it would not be unusual to find my bedding all over the floor along with the contents of the small chest of drawers. Needless to say, I was not late very often after Alexa moved in. She needed a lot of attention and when time allowed we would take her around the zoo; although Jill had more time than I did, I would take her up to the pets' corner, where she was a huge hit with the children. For some reason, however, Alexa had a problem with the two polecat ferrets that were in a large hutch there. She was really nervous of them, curling her lips up and whining softly as she stared at them. As we walked around her eyes remained fixed on them, even to the point of climbing up from my chest, where she would normally be, to my shoulders to look at them. The way she had latched on to them was very strange and eventually we had to cover them up whilst Alexa was there.

Alexa loved company and one of her favourite places was the staff kitchen, where she was a big hit with everybody. She was also spoilt there with the occasional morsel of food. Everyone spent time with her because she was so adorable. She was like a human baby with all their characteristics and it was easy to see why apes and possibly chimps in particular are so close to humans in the evolutionary chain. Alexa had the most gorgeous brown eyes; she was inquisitive but gentle and even when she threw a temper tantrum she was never violent towards us. She would run around and smack the walls of the room and even her face on occasions. Although Gerald Durrell was away more and more as the years went on, he still managed to spend a lot of time with Alexa when he was at the zoo.

My involvement with Alexa reduced a little when Phil and I moved into a flat in St Helier. We were the first keepers to live outside of the zoo in a flat paid for by the trust. I still saw Alexa every day, but as she grew thoughts were developing that she would slowly have to be integrated with the other chimps under close supervision.

I remember taking Alexa to Jersey Pottery for a photo call to advertise the pottery and the zoo. Chumley had performed a similar task when he was young and had caused chaos but, unlike him, Alexa was on her best behaviour. She found the pottery clay interesting and it appeared to taste nice. The flashes from the camera did not disturb her as they had with Chumley; she was as good as gold. On the way back from the pottery Jill was driving and Alexa was sitting on my lap with a paintbrush that she had stolen. Suddenly and without warning, she decided that she wanted to drive. She reached up and grabbed the steering wheel and we very nearly ended up in a field of daffodils, but with all credit to Jill's driving skills, we stayed on the road. I smacked Alexa gently on the hand and she threw a little tantrum and sulked for the rest of the journey, but by the time we arrived at the car park we were friends again. Alexa was a great pal to all the keepers but especially to Jill and me.

Soon after moving into the flat I started to write a children's story about a family of foxes. I had written a similar story when I was younger and this was a revamp of the original entitled *Running Wild*. About a year later I completed it on a tiny portable manual typewriter, having originally written it in longhand. Durrell agreed to read it and make comments, and I was quite chuffed that he was prepared to take time out to read the story, as he was an extremely busy man. He was very kind and encouraging, giving me some tips and constructive comments. He had even made some notes in the draft copy. Taking his advice, I rewrote the entire story and much later. a local paper published it as a serialised story.

Whilst on the subject of books and the media, it was during my time at the zoo that the film *Dr Dolittle* made its debut at a cinema in St Helier. The zoo was approached to see if we could provide an animal for a publicity launch for the film. The decision was made that I would take the blue macaw, Mr Coe, as one did appear in the film. I was decked out in a suit similar to the one worn by Rex Harrison who played Dr Dolittle. We were positioned in the foyer of the cinema and initially I had Mr Coe sitting on my arm but eventually, fearing an accident from his rear, he was placed on a perch next to me. Loads of photographs were taken, and although I did ask for some proofs, they were not forthcoming.; I did, however, receive a complimentary ticket for the film. Mr Coe was well behaved and we had no accidents. I believe he enjoyed the limelight and the titbits he was given. He certainly liked the popcorn but I drew the line at sweets. Of course it was also very useful publicity for the zoo, which Durrell tried to exploit, as it was free.

Mr Coe was also involved in another publicity event when he appeared with 'Miss Jersey' and myself in a photo session under the beautiful archway in front of the main house. I remember our photograph appearing on the front page of the *Jersey Evening Post*. Mr Coe loved all the attention he received on these outings.

You would be forgiven for thinking that I was the only one who did more than just look after our charges, but this was far from the truth. Shep for one was regularly in the paper with his bird-breeding successes. For instance, when the red -thighed falconettes bred for the first time, this appeared on the front page of the *Evening Post*. Both Shep and Durrell were very pleased with this particular event, as it made us the first zoo in Europe to breed these very rare tiny birds of prey. Another cause for a little celebration was in order!

An amusing photograph that could have been taken but was not involved a tiny broody bantam hen that was used as foster mother to five tiny Canada goose goslings. They soon imprinted on her and regarded the hen as their mum. This was fine, until the goslings grew at what seemed to be a tremendous rate. They followed 'Mum' everywhere and it was lovely to watch these large geese towering over the hen and following her in line formation. If only I had owned a camera. then.

Fortunately, there were no cameras around when twelve Indian red-necked parakeets were inadvertently released from their escape-proof aviary – not by me I hasten to add. They did not fly far, in fact they landed in a large oak tree at the swannery where they sat squawking away. Attempts to recapture them by tempting them with food proved useless. After a lot of head scratching, it was decided to try a rocket net that Gerald Durrell had acquired. It was a fairly simple affair, consisting of a huge net that was carried into the air by electrically ignited rockets. The purpose of the net was to catch large flocks of birds for ringing and scientific research, the birds being released as soon as possible after capture. The device was set up with the rockets positioned to carry the net over the tall mature oak. I don't think anyone had considered how we were going to get the birds if the net did not envelop the tree. The net was laid out in front of the tree as the parakeets watched from their lofty perch. Nobody, myself included, had seen the small tree root that the net had been laid over, and this was to have some significance. I mused over the possibility that once everything was in place the birds might just fly off.

By the time everything was organised we had attracted quite an audience of staff but fortunately no visitors. The staff from the office and cafeteria had all come down to watch. Once we were set and at the countdown of three, the ignition was fired and up went the rockets with a *whoosh* trailing the fine net behind. Up it went and the birds remained perched. Suddenly, the net snagged on the tree root, the net stretched tightly and this had the effect of pulling the rockets back in a big arc over the keepers. We stood there well and truly netted and a roar of laughter ensued, not only from the audience but also from us as we tried to extricate ourselves. I was in absolute hysterics. The fine netting had hooked on to everything and it took us quite a while to get free. I am sure the parakeets were laughing at us.

Despite further offers of food, our efforts failed and they were free flying around the zoo and ultimately the island. To add insult to injury they had failed to breed whilst in captivity but once free it was a different story. The mild climate of the island had obviously helped. It was a fact that amused Durrell. But could he claim it as a breeding success? The keeper who released them certainly did not get the credit!

With the breeding concept being of paramount importance for the zoo, an issue that perplexed Durrell and Jeremy during my time there revolved around the great apes. The chimpanzees were breeding despite the difficulty with Alexa; however, Oscar and Bali had not been successful, although Bali had previously had a miscarriage. The main problem involved the gorillas, N'Pongo and Nandy, both females with no male. It was proving virtually impossible to locate a male but eventually, after I had left, a male, Jambo, was found and brought to the zoo and a successful breeding group was established. Jambo was, of course, famous for protecting the child that fell into the gorilla enclosure from the females, until the child was rescued. I never had the privilege of meeting him but understood from people who worked with him that he was a gentle giant. A bronze statue of Jambo now stands near the enclosure following his death.

We used to trade a lot of animals with other zoos in those early days, with the benefits being felt all around. I particularly remember that many of our young birds of prey were sent to the Welsh Mountain Zoo and a male Canadian otter was sent to us from Basle Zoo in Switzerland to establish a breeding programme with our two females, Mungles and Chips. A new enclosure was built next to the arch near the staff kitchen. The otter's pool was glass fronted, enabling visitors to see the animals swimming under water, and this proved to be a very popular feature, particularly for the children. Otters are really one of the most endearing of creatures, their playful nature and apparent joy for life sets them apart from many mammals.

There was a constant stream of animals and birds in and out of the zoo, as breeding programmes were established involving more and more different species. It made life very interesting for the keepers and as the number of 'firsts' increased, the parties became more frequent. One breeding success I will always remember, as I was directly involved in the birth: we had a lovely pair of leopards, Lokai the male and Gerda the female. After a few years of inactivity on the breeding front, they successfully bred for the first time. Martin was in charge of the big cats and, whilst Gerda was fine with the keepers, Lokai was not to be trusted. As the birth drew near, it was decided to separate the cats, as it was felt that Lokai might pose a threat to the newborn cubs, as is often the case with some big cats in the wild.

Eventually, the day arrived. Gerda had been pacing up and down inside the sleeping section and getting up and down in the bedding. She was generally very restless. At lunch time, Quentin noticed that she was lying down and panting heavily. When he and Martin went in and examined her, they discovered that the first cub was breeched. Its tail appeared to be out but the remainder of the cub was stuck. A vet was requested and attended. I went in with Quentin, Martin and the vet, who, with delicate manipulation, managed to turn the cub and almost immediately it came out. What a wonderful moment that was! We stayed with Gerda as three more cubs were born and the experience was wonderful. Gerda cleaned them up and, having checked that all was well, we left her to her new babies. The cubs were just like their parents and grew quickly, becoming another popular attraction for the visitors. There was cause for a major celebration that evening.

It was not long after that incredible birth that we had another in the bedroom next to mine. Shep's Alsatian Reema gave birth one evening to thirteen pups. We thought this was a record at the time. The pups were gorgeous and grew up at the zoo with the Leopard leopard cubs. We had other dogs at the zoo; Jeremy had a very large basset hound and a boxer; there was a black Labrador, though but I can't remember who owned that, and an Airedale terrier, in addition to Shep's two. There was an amusing photograph in the staff kitchen with all the dogs lined up in front of a wall looking at the camera.

In the pets' corner the two polecat ferrets that we thought were both male jacks had bred, and as the young grew they became very popular with the visitors, as constant handling had made them tame like their parents. Other animals in the pets' corner included some miniature Dutch rabbits that were very attractive, mice and guinea pigs. One of the stars was an umbrella-crested cockatoo named Twirpy who was pure white and very pretty. She would talk to the children, which caused great hilarity. She had quite an extensive repertoire, although her favourite party trick was to dance on her perch. All you had to do was say, 'Twirpy, dance,' and she would start bobbing her head up and down. As she got into the dance her whole body would be bobbing and her magnificent crest would stand up. Faster and faster she would go, screeching as the dance reached its peak. It was at this point that she would completely forget herself and fall backwards off her perch on to the bottom of the cage, about nine inches below, where she would lay motionless with her feet sticking up in the air. She would stay there until picked up. I would then place her on my shoulder and she would push her head into my neck in an affectionate way. She would do this to the visitors as well if placed on their shoulders. On a busy day she would sometimes perform this dance up to three times. Shep believed that she was about seventy years old and he also thought that the dance was some form of sexual display, although he was not certain. If I had the time to do it and if there were enough visitors in pets' corner, I would start Twirpy off, and as she reached the peak I would put my open hands below the perch and catch her as she fell. She always looked dead but soon perked up as I placed her on an excited child's shoulder, and she would show her affection. She would often tickle the child's neck, prompting uncontrollable giggling and securing her place as a firm favourite.

I once suggested to Jeremy that we should put Asia in the pets' corner so that she could swear at the visitors and the children in particular. I would have loved to see their reaction. Needless to say my idea was not welcomed with open arms and I received a very rude reply. (I can't think why!). I always found it curious that with all the colourful, majestic and fascinating animals at the zoo, the children always made for the pets' corner as soon as they were through the entrance gate. I suppose it was the possibility of a hands-on experience.

Chumley, our magnificent male chimpanzee, was a constant source of amusement to the keepers, but often at the visitors' expense. He had a very unsociable habit that involved the public, particularly in the summer when the chimps' outside enclosure would draw big crowds. Chumley had a real dislike of cameras, in particular cine-cameras (videos were still a long way off then). Because the main diet for the chimps was fruit and vegetables, their droppings were generally fairly loose. Despite being cleaned out daily, their droppings would get integrated into the thin layer of sawdust on the floor. When a suitable number of visitors had gathered and the cameras were rolling, Chumley would stand up on his back legs and start to wind himself up. The dark hair would stand up on his shoulders and he would start making a soft low 'woow' call; at the same time he would be gathering up some droppings and sawdust with his hands and making it into a ball. The 'woow' would get louder and louder and he would rock backwards and forwards. When the rocking started the females retired to their inside quarters; they knew what was about to happen. Suddenly the 'woow' would turn into a screech and Chumley would gather up the ball as he rushed forward screaming at the top of his voice. He would run to the bars and with an underarm swing he would hurl his handful at an unsuspecting visitor that he had targeted earlier in the proceedings. His accuracy would have been the pride of any England fast bowler. The victim would often be covered but it was usually the camera that would get the full force of the projectile. This was the moment for us to disappear if we had been in the vicinity and avoid the inevitable complaint.

I can vividly recall one incident involving Chumley. I was helping Phil in the kitchen of the ape house one hot, sunny summer's day and the zoo was packed. All of a sudden we heard Chumley start his soft 'woow' noise. We rushed outside to try and warn the large crowd that he was about to throw something that would not be very pleasant through the bars, but we were totally ignored. We disappeared inside and shut the door. We could hear Chumley winding up and the 'woow' sound was getting louder. Finally, there was the familiar screech, which was matched by an almost identical one from the crowd. Phil and I just looked at each other and shrugged our shoulders.

Shortly afterwards there was a knock at the kitchen door despite the 'Staff Only' sign outside. I opened the door and there stood Chumley's latest victim. The young woman was in tears and the reason was obvious. She was covered from head to foot with Chumley's present. Her long blonde hair was matted over her face and her bright bright yellow summer dress was absolutely ruined. Her boyfriend stood next to her still holding the cine-camera that was also plastered. Phil and I both thought that this must have been a record handful that Chumley had thrown. I took them to the office, and on the way I was tempted to remind them that they had been warned, but I felt this might not be appropriate under the circumstances. In addition, the boyfriend was about six foot six, built like a rugby player and was already very unhappy. I kept my distance from them both, as the smell was quite strong. The woman was cleaned up and offered some recompense for the inconvenience, although I should add that this was not offered every time.

As Chumley developed the dominant male role, albeit the only male, he would perform this routine three or four times per day and it was therefore decided to put up a large sign outside warning visitors that the chimps may throw things. In addition, we placed some sheets of clear plastic along the bottom of the barrier to offer some protection. A further warning was placed in the visitors' guide. Interestingly, Chumley was the only individual among the great apes that we had that threw anything.

A further incident involving visitor/animal contact was quite amusing, from my point of view at least. At the time I was helping Malcolm prepare some feeds in the kitchen of the small mammal house. The large kitchen window gave us a clear view of the central corridor leading down between the various enclosures and it was in this corridor that the visitors used to look at the animals. In the middle of the house to the left when looking down from the kitchen and next to Polly and the ring-tailed lemurs was an enclosure containing two celebes monkeys that were notorious for grabbing. They went for glasses, visitors' guides and whatever else took their fancy. There was a sign warning visitors of this fact.

On this particular day there was a gentleman of senior years, smartly dressed and who obviously had money, with a very voluptuous blonde girl on his arm who was evidently a lot younger than him. She was quite stunning with a remarkable figure and I remember thinking how lucky the man was. It was quite apparent that they were not father and daughter, particularly in the way they were whispering to each other and giggling. Also they were taking a lot more interest in each other than they were in the animals that they had allegedly come to see. They were walking towards the kitchen when suddenly as they reached the celebes' enclosure a black arm shot out and, quick as a flash, grabbed the man's hair and pulled it off. Instantly, two black arms were pulling the toupee through the wire and into the enclosure. The girl let out an almighty scream and looked in shocked horror at the man. I am certain that she had not previously realised that he had a hairpiece. His bald head was gleaming in the bright lights and the expression on her face was of total disbelief, surprise and astonishment. He stood in abject horror as he watched his hair disappearing into the monkey's enclosure. I must admit that I had not spotted that he was wearing a toupee but the monkey obviously had.

The couple left immediately before I could speak to them, whilst the monkeys were merrily tearing their prize into small pieces. Malcolm had been out when the incident occurred and when he came back we pondered the possibility of retrieving the hairpiece, but we decided that it was going to be more trouble than it was worth. It was the monkeys' prize and they were not going to give it up easily. I let the office know what had happened, as I was certain that the couple would have reported the matter, but they had not. I was asked to try and find them. I checked at the main entrance and was told that they had left in a hurry, apparently having a row. They had roared out of the car park leaving a cloud of dust and we never saw or heard from them again.

Malcolm eventually managed to recover the remains of the toupee when the monkeys finally lost interest in it. They had ripped it into tiny shreds. To avoid any further incidents, as it was feared somebody might actually be hurt, a wire mesh was placed over the existing wire, thereby preventing black arms from reaching out. Eventually the monkeys were moved to a much larger enclosure outside.

This was the story throughout the zoo. As funds became available, new enclosures, aviaries and pens were constructed to improve the 'hotel' accommodation. The small mammal house, the bird house, the binturong enclosure, along with the bear, baboon and quarantine sections, were all conversions of the existing manor house buildings. It was an exciting time as the zoo developed and grew. I helped Jill with a major refurbishment of the vivariums and pens. There was a pair of tuatara, a very rare ancient species of lizard from New Zealand, that had a handsome spiked mane, which extended almost the full length of their two-foot long body. Attempts to breed them had so far proved unsuccessful, so they were moved into their own large open circular pen on the floor in the centre of the reptile house; they had previously shared a pen with some tortoises. Other residents of the reptile house were a pair of deadly poisonous copper head snakes and a variety of pythons and boas including an eighteen-foot long reticulated python called, strangely enough, Retic. There was also a blue-tongued skink that was so shaped that it was difficult to tell initially which end was its head and which its tail. At eighteen-inches long, he was very solid and heavy and had thick scales all over his body. As the name suggests, he had a beautiful blue tongue with a sharp and powerful jaw that could give a nasty bite.

I recall one incident in the reptile house when I was helping Jill change the turfs in some of the vivariums. These were changed about every two weeks, with fresh ones being dug from the bank above the swannery and the old ones being planted back on the bank. They soon recovered and grew – a recycling programme that worked very well. A nice flat turf was placed in one of the pythons' vivariums in the corner, to provide fresh cover and a new patch to explore and investigate. A few days later Jill called me down to the reptile house to show me something. There in the python's vivarium with the new flat turf, sliding through the grass was a six-inch grass snake. As we watched it, the baby snake slid over the larger five-foot python that was coiled partly under the turf. It appeared to ignore the intruder completely. Jill removed it without much difficulty, and after showing it to one or two members of staff, it was released back on to the bank above the swannery – a good area for it with the nearby water. We can only assume that it was in the turf when it was dug, as the vivarium's glass sliding fronts are locked to avoid unwanted attention particularly with the copper heads.

On my eighteenth birthday I became the proud owner of a boneshaker of a motorcycle that was my first form of transport on the island. Prior to that I had been dependent on other zoo members or friends for lifts into St Helier. Of course, this was before Phil and I moved into the town. It was a 250cc Villiers engine mounted on a very heavy pale blue BMW frame. The complete machine weighed a ton but at the end of the day it was transport, which gave me a little freedom. I believe it cost me fifty pounds, which was a lot of money in those days and a fortune to me. The wages were understandably very low at the zoo and we worked for the love of the job more than money.

The motorcycle gave me the chance to go off on the rare occasions when we had free time. I would take the binoculars and marmite sandwiches of course and go off bird watching. Winter was better than summer with less visitors on the beaches and cliffs. One of my favourite places were the cliffs, rocks and beach at Le Tacq at the western end of the island, the north end of St Ouens Bay, a magnificent five mile long sandy bay. Guillemots, cormorants and a host of seagulls frequented this area in the winter. With curlew and oystercatchers on the fields and grass above Le Tacq, it was a majestic place to just sit and watch. In the summer, visitors such as wood warbler, willow and garden warbler joined these birds, and in particular the sedge warbler, that regularly nested in the patches of dense bramble at the base of the cliffs. Swifts would regularliy nest, if you can call it that, towards the tops of the cliffs, and I have always been fascinated with the fulmars that used to nest in the same area. They would glide on out stretched wings on the strong breezes that were a regular feature of this part of the Jersey coastline. They would spiral effortlessly just above the waves, no matter how rough, and would very rarely flap their wings, arriving from the open ocean where they had wandered throughout the long winter until mid-April purely to breed, by the end of August they were usually gone. They have a unique defence strategy if threatened: they spit a horrible green fluid at the aggressor, which smells awful. I actually witnessed this once at Le Tacq when I was watching a pair that had nested, with the old, faithful binoculars. I was watching a jackdaw that appeared to be getting nearer the pair who were sitting tight. Finally, their patience ran out and when the thief was close enough, he was showered with the green fluid.

The jackdaw flew off, shaking himself violently to remove the foul smelling liquid and I never saw him return to pester the fulmars again. Some time after this I was to witness the same defence used on a very intrusive photographer to very good effect, but that comes later.

It was also at Le Tacq that I saw my first Jersey bank vole, a tiny rodent similar to the voles found on the mainland but slightly smaller and paler. When Phil and I moved to the flat in St Helier, he commenced a scientific study of the Jersey bank vole and we had vivariums dotted around the flat and at the zoo containing pairs of voles. They became part of our lives; they were quite fascinating creatures and most endearing with their blunt noses, short tails and bulging eyes. The study Phil was undertaking was a long-term investigation into their breeding, behaviour, diet, life cycle and anything else of interest. This research project was still in progress when I left the zoo but Phil did publish a scientific paper at the end of the study. They remain rare and the only indigenous rodent on the island.

In those early days the zoo was open for 364 days of the year, shutting only on Christmas Day. Christmas was always great fun at the zoo:, the staff kitchen was decorated and we had a small Christmas tree in the corner with the obligatory lights on. There was a wonderful atmosphere in the kitchen, which was also the staff's First Aid centre, drying room, staff room and most importantly bar. Although the zoo was closed for Christmas Day, it was business as usual as far as feeding, cleaning and general welfare of the animals was concerned. The only difference was that it was a little accelerated and non-essential tasks were left. Everybody mucked in (no pun intended) and helped each other. If one keeper finished early, they would help out in other sections.

I think that every Christmas during my time at the zoo something of significance happened. One year, Malcolm's tamarins decided to produce babies on Christmas morning, which, I suppose, was rather apt really. Another year Claudius decided to go walkabout, having broken down the fence of the paddock. It was after our Christmas meal, so you can imagine the sight of an assemblage of keepers all wearing funny paper hats and tinsel going after Claudius. However, it obviously had the desired effect because as soon as he saw us, he wandered back to the paddock with only the minimum of encouragement from us. Somebody suggested that maybe we should look ridiculous a bit more often, and someone else retorted that we already did. Claudette and Juno remained in the paddock, despite the gaping hole that Claudius had made which had to be swiftly repaired.

A further Christmas saw one of Frisky's females give birth a week early. The plan was to separate Frisky, to prevent him harming the infant, and of course this plan had to be brought forward but was completed with very little difficulty. One Christmas Eve a New Guinea singing dog decided to whelp with five lovely puppies, but at the same time the dominant male, or alpha male to be correct, became seriously ill. He was removed from their enclosure and placed in the quarantine section and a vet was called. He was none too happy at being called out on Christmas Eve but he diagnosed the dog as suffering from a virus, which he recovered from within a few days. So Christmas was always and eventful and interesting time but very enjoyable, helped along with plenty of Christmas ale, of course.

In contrast to the comparative quiet of the winter months with only a trickle of visitors, the spring and summer were always busy. The early spring would see the honeymoon couples that thronged to the island in April and May – not that they were always interested in the animals and birds as they walked around. At weekends in high summer it was often difficult to get around the zoo due to the volume of visitors and we all had what I can only describe as problem visitors from time to time. The biggest headache were the group of lads that would arrive having consumed copious amounts of alcohol in a local pub and often with cans in their hands as they wandered around. On one occasion there was a small group of lads obviously under the influence, outside the orang-utan's outside quarters. They were very loud, shouting at Oscar and Bali, who were not impressed. Phil was watching them from a discreet distance when he saw one of the youths throw a can at Bali. The can fell well within Oscar's reach and as quick as a flash he went for it but Phil managed to get there first. (The trouble Oscar could get into with a can does not bear thinking about.) Phil spoke politely to the group but received a barrage of abuse in return. Word was passed around amongst the keepers to be on the lookout for this group, and sure enough in the reptile house they tried to wake up Retic the python by banging really hard on the glass front of his enclosure. Jill asked them to leave, and after another mouthful of abuse they did. It was then decided that we could not tolerate any further incidents with this group, so a few keepers assembled and the lads were asked to leave the zoo. Despite some initial objections, they decided that a confrontation with the keepers might not be in their best interests and they were escorted off the zoo premises. As they entered the car park one of the group demanded his money back but the look he received from us answered him. They sped out of the car park in a cloud of dust.

The zoo operated a policy of visitors not feeding the residents. This was brought in to enable zoo staff to maintain a balanced and healthy diet for all of our charges. There were signs all around the zoo reminding visitors of this policy and explaining the reasons for it. It also appeared in the zoo guide, but despite this there would always be one person who would sneak food in and try it on. Normally, a firm talking to was all that was needed; however, I remember an occasion when we had 'Mr and Mrs Objectionable' in with their two children, who were miniatures of their parents. They had entered the zoo with three loaves of bread in a bag, which had gone undetected by the girl on the entrance turnstile. They were first discovered feeding the apes with bread.

N'Pongo and Oscar thought it was great fun. The family was firmly told not to feed any of the animals and the reasons for this. Further round the zoo they were caught feeding the colobus monkeys and were again asked not to feed the animals. The third occasion they were throwing large pieces of bread to Frisky the baboon and at that point they were told to leave the zoo. Initially they refused on the grounds that they had paid to come in. It was pointed out that paying to come in did not allow them to break the zoo rules. They still refused to leave and walked off throwing bread around in a confrontational manner. The troops were massed and descended on the family who were escorted promptly off the premises. I should point out that these types of incidents were very rare but as keepers it was something that had to be borne in mind; the welfare of the animals in our charge was of paramount importance.

We had no dedicated security officers at that time and would take it in turns to walk around the zoo before retiring at night, to ensure that all was well. The car park had no gates, which allowed unrestricted access to the public and was therefore checked every night. Courting couples regularly frequented the car park after dark but a quick flash of the torch would send them scurrying out; however, some of the sights were interesting, to say the least.

It was during my time at Jersey Zoo that I developed an interest in photography. With my cheap Kodak camera I took some good photographs, one in particular of the cereopsis geese. Sadly, however, over the years I have lost most of my early photos, but as you will read later, photography was to become a major part of my life.

By way of conclusion to this chapter, we can look at the tremendous success that the zoo has achieved in the three decades since I left. Despite the scepticism of biologists and zoologists in the early years, it is now world renowned for its breeding programme of endangered species. In 1973 Durrell formed the Wildlife Preservation Trust International, based in Philadelphia, Pennsylvania. In 1985 a further affiliate joined the group – the Wildlife Preservation Trust Canada, based in Toronto. The three groups were collectively known as The Wildlife Preservation Trusts.

Sadly, Gerald Durrell died in 1995 but in his last few years it must have pleased him to see how successful the trust had become. As we move towardsare in the Millennium, the trust have decided as a fitting tribute to the work of the great man to rename the Jersey trust The Durrell Wildlife Conservation Trust.

I started this chapter with a quote from Durrell which appears in the Trust's Red Book and I will finish with a second quote that comes from the Register of Bequests 1988--1998. 'I'm glad to be giving something back to this earth because I've been so extraordinarily lucky and had such great pleasure from it.' Gerald Durrell

In 1969 I became restless for a change. I was twenty years old and wanted to travel. I had become friendly with a group of local lads of the same age and we all felt the same way. Shep knew that I was becoming fidgety and one day he and I had a real heart to heart. I was desperately torn between my love for the zoo and the urge to travel. I suppose in hindsight I was impetuous but I had to get it out of my system – that was basically the advice that Shep gave me. So in the autumn of that year and with very mixed emotions, I left the zoo and moved to France with a good mate, Richard Prouten. As a leaving present, Durrell gave me a boxed set of his books with an autographed card, which has remained one of my most prized possessions.

Many years after I left the zoo I learned from Shep that Oscar had died of colitis soon after I moved to France and his mate had died some time later. Alexa went to John Aspinall's zoo in Kent where she had a baby, which she successfully reared before Alexa herself died some years later. George Jacobs eventually ended up as an Eelephant keeper at Aspinall's and wrote a fabulous book entitled *'Memoirs of a Coarse Zoo Keeper'*. Jill Watson left and went to Zimbabwe. Martin Carslake also left but is still working in the conservation field. Stefan Ormorod worked for the RSPCA for many years but sadly died recently. Phil Coffey left for a career in teaching. Shep retired in 1997 but maintains links with the zoo as a consultant. Quentin Bloxham is now the zoo programme director, and Jeremy the zoo director having been awarded the OBE in 1998 for lifelong work in international conservation. The chimpanzees were eventually moved to another zoo to make room for an enlarged orang-utan enclosure. About two weeks after being moved, a keeper left their enclosure door open and the chimps escaped. Each had to be darted with a powerful tranquilliser to recapture them. Tragically, Chumley was given too much of the drug and died.

Over the thirty years since I left the zoo, it has become internationally renowned for its breeding programmes and is now the Rolls-Royce of zoos.

As the zoo has moved on, so must I, to another chapter of my life.

En France

The recollections in this chapter are drawn from a journal that I kept during our stay in France.

Having landed at St Malo with our Mini, we drove to Rouen, where as luck would have it there was a big beer festival in progress hosted by one of the major French lager companies. We had a great time before bedding down in our tent, which we had pitched in amongst some bushes in the middle of nowhere, or so we thought. The following morning we were woken at 5 a.m. by the sound of the tent shaking violently and voices outside shouting, 'Anglais, Anglais.' We must have looked bewildered as we peered out of the tent with bleary eyes and very sore heads. The scene that greeted us brought us to our senses at a glance – six gendarmes who did not look at all happy surrounded us. The reason was that we had pitched the tent on the central reservation of a major dual carriageway and traffic was racing past in both directions, swerving around our car that was parked in the road nearby. That was the quickest ever time that the tent was packed away, and I promptly learned to soft talk French policemen in French – welcome to France.

With very sore hangovers and suffering from the after-effects of an early morning, we drove to Paris, (what a beautiful city). We spent almost four weeks there, staying with one of Richard's uncles. We did all of the sights from the Eiffel Tower to the basilique du Sacré-Coeur and Montmartre – which was one of my favourite regions of the city. But with money dwindling we eventually had to move on, basically to find work.

Stopping off briefly at Fontainebleau to see the spectacular palace, we headed south through Sens, Joigny, Auxerre, Vermenton, Avallon and Saulieu, before eventually arriving at Chalon, where we stayed for two days. Continuing south we drove through vineyards that stretched as far as the eye could see, and after passing through a tiny village called Lagnieu, we started ascending into the mountains. This was my first visit to a mountainous region and I was awe struck by the beauty. There were diminutive villages perched on the side of the mountain. On one of the frequent stops to let the engine and brakes cool, and to stretch our legs, I almost stepped on an adder that was basking on a rocky path. I don't know who was more startled. Another of these stops was next to a mountain stream with crystal-clear water that tasted sweet and fresh. A dipper flew past my head and landed on a rock nearby, bobbing up and down. Suddenly, it dived into the water and seconds later reappeared on the same stone with a small insect in its beak. The bird repeated this two or three times before flying further up the stream. In the heart of the mountains, we saw numerous buzzards soaring high above the peaks. Mountain hares, one of the buzzard's main prey, were bounding between the rocks and occasionally ran across the road in front of us. A host of autumn flowering plants were oin flower but I could not identify them; however, the air was full of the scent of herbs such as thyme and sage. We slept in the car for two days and lived on French bread and pâté, which we bought daily at the boulangerie in the village. I can think of worse diets.

We eventually descended a steep valley that played havoc with our brakes, which continually overheated, but finally we entered the town of Grenoble that nestled in the mountains with a beautiful river running through the middle. I spotted a cable car going up the side of the mountain over the river, and having established that the return fare was four francs, we had to go. I had never been in a cable car before and am not the best with heights, but I'm glad I went, as it was tremendous. The view from the top was absolutely spectacular. The car had dropped us off at a building at the top known as the Bastille, where we had a panoramic view of the town and you could clearly see the old part as well as the relatively new section, We learned that Grenoble was preparing for the 1969 Winter Olympics. From the Bastille we could see the ski slopes in the distance, which, of course, were still devoid of snow. Having watched buzzards high above us in the mountains, it was interesting to see a pair soaring above the town but below where we were standing.

The descent appeared to be a lot quicker. Every time we passed one of the supporting towers, the car dropped like a stone and our stomachs were in our mouths. Once we had recovered from the trip down we had a meal and then drove back into the mountains, pitched the tent under a tree and then cracked open and polished off a bottle of *vin ordinaire*. All night we heard gentle thudding sounds coming from the roof of the tent but we chose to ignore them. The following morning we found the outer edge of the tent to be deep in green walnuts. We filled our long white woollen socks with the nuts, which we feasted on for some time afterwards. We had the car serviced in Grenoble and then continued going south-west and eventually reached a tiny village called Villa de Lens, nestling in a valley surrounded by a massif of mountains. We both fell in love with the place; it was as if time stood still. We had travelled over a thousand miles and passed through numerous charming villages, particularly in the mountains, but none were as attractive as this one. After taking a walk around the village, we discovered that there was a sawmill which employed most of the villagers, but unfortunately there was no work for us and our funds were critically low.

We slept in the car; it was my turn to sleep in the front

with my feet out of the window, and I awoke to find my socks covered in frost the following morning.

We continued south-west and into what appeared to be the heart of the Alps. The air was thin; so thin in fact that we had to remove the thermostat from the Mini's cooling system as the altitude was affecting the engine, which resulted in it regularly overheating. We were by now several thousand feet up and even we were feeling it. The white houses in the villages stood out against the starkness of the barren surroundings. One particular village called Jonchères was perched on the peak of a mountain overlooking a deep valley, where another village called Die nestled. These villages were so isolated that the effect of winter and the snow did not bear thinking about. Finally, we reached the small town of Nyon and at this point in the journey the mileage gauge on the car was indicating that we had travelled fifteen hundred miles since landing at St Malo.

Just after Nyon, the mountains came to a fairly abrupt end and we entered another grape district. We spent a night in the car outside Bagnols where French stick and pâté were the order of the day again. I remember this village, for as we sat and tucked into the food, a cock chaffinch was so bold as to take morsels of bread from my hand and having finished with me he scrounged from Richard. The following night was spent at Alès where we had a hot meal – the first for a few days. In the small restaurant we feasted on a quite delicious casserole, which we later learned consisted of goat!

We were now entering the region of Provence and this was to have a profound effect on me. We stopped at the town of Arles where we learned that there might be work apple picking on a local farm. This was good news as we were down to our last few francs. We slept in the car and drove to the farm early the next morning. Richard spoke to the farm foreman, as his French was better than mine. We were in luck and there was work picking the Golden Delicious apples at three francs fifty cents per hour. The wages were not exorbitant but it was money and we were also offered free accommodation and the luxury of a bed, which after the discomfort of the car, made our decision academic. We started the following day at 7 a.m. and finished at 6 p.m. These hours were designed to avoid the plagues of mosquitoes that came out in their millions. We had oil to repel them but they still managed to get under your clothes. Richard appeared to suffer more than I did – I think I have rhino skin. There was a lot of water around with rice being grown in shallow flooded fields all around the eighty-acre orchard that we were working in. All this water provided a perfect breeding ground for insects. The trees were not very tall and were full of tiny green tree frogs that merrily fed on the mosquitoes. The frogs were about one and a half inches fully grown and the adults had a bright yellow stripe down the inside of the back legs. We had been warned about the frogs but not about the snakes that moved amongst the trees feeding on them. These were also green, non-poisonous and about eighteen inches long in their adult state.

Each evening we would drive to a nearby village, Le Sombuc, for a meal, and I remember once we had the casserole of the day, which was really tasty with a strong wine flavour. After we had finished we enquired what the delicious meat was. The patron told us it was 'renard' – yes, fox! Richard went very pale.

Another evening we were returning from the restaurant and about to enter our accommodation when I spotted a large brown preying mantis under the porch. It was about five inches long and rocking gently in the breeze. We gave it a wide berth. The size of some of the other creatures gave cause for concern. There were large wasps about one and a half inches long, often flying through the trees to hunt. Huge dragonflies would do the same with their beautiful bright colours ranging from brilliant blue to a vivid scarlet. One particular dragonfly was a dull brown, but at five inches long it was by far the biggest. You could hear it coming from quite a distance away and it would regularly hover deep in the trees.

Buzzards would hunt over and amongst the trees and I once saw one take a water vole off the surface of one of the rice fields – a spectacular sight! I also saw an egret feeding in the water of one of the ditches that straddled the orchard.

Once we had settled into the routine and got some money behind us, we would go off and explore the region on the Sundays when we did not have to work. We spent most of our free time driving further south into the heart of the Camargue – an area I had first heard of whilst at the zoo as a very important area for conservation.

The Camargue is an alluvial plain on the Rhône Delta. It is some 367 square miles and was formed by the actions of the Rhône River, the Mediterranean Sea and the wind. It is a truly wild place, being flat as the eye can see and covered with sparse salt tolerant vegetation such as sea lavender, tamarisk, glasswort and reeds. Trees were scarce but a few willow and alder had established in the drier areas. Sandbanks were the remnant of salt extraction and provided perfect nest sites for sand martins and bee-eaters. Some of the sandbanks were riddled with holes but the birds had departed. This vast wild marshy area boasts some four hundred species of birds, of which one hundred and sixty are migratory such as the bee-eater. The region also provides wintering grounds for birds from the arctic tundra such as the diminutive teal that descend on the region in huge flocks. We used to watch them fly up in flocks silhouetted against the beautiful red sunset.

The white egret, purple and grey heron and cormorant were all taking advantage of the excellent fishing with bream, carp, perch, pike and especially eel. A few terns were still feeding up before migrating and swallows and house martins were making the most of the mosquitoes before they flew south. Bearded tits moved effortlessly amongst the reeds and came quite close to us. They are the most attractive of the tit-mouse family.

However, the bird that the Camargue is famous for more than any other is the greater flamingo. These beautiful and spectacular birds feed on the tiny shellfish; they are filter feeders and a very ancient form of bird. We only saw a few while we were there, which were paler than the birds we had had at the zoo. To see them in the wild was a magical experience.

The other animals that this region is renowned for are the small, black wild bulls that roam free all over the Camargue. They are rounded up and used in the famous Provençal bull-fights, but unlike the Spanish bullfights, these bulls are not killed at the end of the contest. Wild horses also roamed freely; these are small, strong animals that are predominantly grey in colour. It is believed that they are directly descended from a prehistoric animal whose bones were unearthed at a huge horse cemetery near Lyon. The people of the Camargue revere them for their stamina, intelligence and spirit. The foals, of which we saw quite a few, are born brown and only turn grey at four or five years of age. To see these lovely horses galloping in a herd through the shallow water in the sunlight was a sight I will never forget.

Despite searching for them we never saw any otter, racoon or beaver, all three of which can be found in the region. Water voles were the most common mammal we saw during our stay there. In the streams around the orchard and in the shallow pools further into the region, we saw small aquatic tortoise known locally as *cistardos*. Green lizards also abounded in the drier areas. These were quite beautiful, bright green with brown speckled diamond-shaped markings running down their sides. At almost nine inches long, they were much larger than the common and sand lizards found in Britain.

The autumn breeze would blow through the reed beds disturbing the reed and sedge warblers that had stopped off to feed on their passage to Southern Africa. The mosquitoes provided a much needed and plentiful food supply.

One evening I found a bright green praying mantis on the side of the lane. It was smaller than the one we had seen at the farm, and as I watched, it soon became apparent that it was hunting a grasshopper in the grass ahead of it. The mantis was rocking menacingly as it very slowly crept towards its victim. Fortunately for the grasshopper it jumped away before becoming a snack.

Everywhere you looked wildlife was busy. Whether it was early morning, afternoon or evening, there was always something to see. I could not spend enough time there but work was also very important.

After almost four weeks at the farm, the apples were finished and it was time to move on. We collected our pay and drove south-west to Albaron and then to the Mediterranean at Stes-Maries-de-la-Mer. We parked up right next to the sea and spent the night in the car missing the comfortable bed at the farm already. We woke to the beautiful sound of skylarks singing in the blue sky high above the car. We drove back to Albaron and then east around the main expanse of water known as Etang de Vaccarès and around Salin-de-Badon, and it was here that we saw one of the most beautiful sunsets we had seen whilst in France. It had been clear all day and, as the sun set in the west, the red glow was spectacular and a perfect reflection on the lake. As the sun sank below the horizon, shafts of red light shot up into the darkening sky – an exquisite end to our stay, for the following day we headed east and away from the Camargue, an area of truly outstanding natural beauty and one that is now an internationally protected area as one of the jewels of France.

As we drove east looking for work we passed over the River Rhône and from the bridge we could see hundreds of waders on the mud flats and on the banks. Small flocks of knot and dunlin were scuttling around probing the mud with their short beaks for worms and other insects. Oystercatchers were at the top of the bank, their long bright red beaks glistening in the sun. A few turnstones were on the water's edge but the most magnificent birds we saw were the large curlews with their resplendently long curling beaks probing deep into the mud for the crustaceans that the other birds could not reach. We had heard the haunting call of the curlew both at the farm and in the marshes but had not seen them before.

The second night after leaving the farm was spent at Aix-en-Provence. After a good meal in the town we slept in the car, which came hard after the luxury of the bed at the farm. Even worse was the fact that it was my turn to sleep in the front with my feet out, but a violent thunderstorm and very heavy rain all night prevented me from opening the window and it took quite a while for the circulation to re-establish the next morning. A typical French breakfast of a bowl of black coffee and French bread followed by croissants set us up for the day. We drove to St Raphael, and as it was so hot, we went for a swim in the sea, which was a wonderful crystal-clear blue. Reluctantly, we had to leave the sea and continue on our quest for work. We went along the coast to Cannes and soon discovered that this was the expensive area, and with our limited funds we could not afford to linger. We drove on to Nice. It was 26 October and Picasso's eighty-seventh birthday. The whole city appeared to be celebrating and it was even in the newspapers. We made a few enquiries for work and discovered that the farm work was north-west of Nice, around the town of Grasse, so off we went, arriving at the outskirts of Grasse at dusk. After another night in the car, we drew a blank but were told that they were still grape picking on a farm near Antibes, so back we went down to the coast.

At Antibes we found a small vineyard that was still hiring pickers. We spent a week there finishing off the grape harvest. The season of grape picking, the *vendanges*, was finally over. Apart from one or two warblers in amongst the vines and the occasional buzzard soaring overhead, we did not see very much, especially after the bottle of wine that all the pickers were given at lunch time, after which we could hardly see the grapes! The owner of the vineyard had two sons who had studied agriculture in England and really wanted to help us. He contacted a friend of his at Digne in the Basses-Alpes and secured work for us for a few weeks. We left the farm and drove through the mountains that looked really spectacular in the moonlight, with the peaks silhouetted in the star-filled night sky. But driving at night through the mountains can be quite hair-raising; there are sheer drops into blackness with nothing to stop the car going over in many places. Another night in the car, and my socks poking out of the window were covered in frost the following morning. We had breakfast in the town and then drove to the farm in the charming little village of Les Meese, which was about seventeen miles from Digne. We drove over one mountain called le Mont Ventoux with an altitude of 1,912 metres. The weather was bitterly cold with a biting north-easterly wind, but the view from the peak was quite spectacular, with lavender fields extending almost as far as the eye could see. We arrived at the farm and met the owner, Monsieur Richard. Work started the following day and our accommodation this time was a converted milking shed – a bit damp but more comfortable than the car!

The work was in the huge expanse of glasshouses that formed the bulk of the farm, and we were working in *les salades*, mainly lettuces. Richard prepared the peat for planting, whilst I was in another section pricking out lettuce plants in their thousands. It was back-breaking but it was work. Being separated from Richard, my French improved dramatically. Up until this time I could only speak some pidgin French and had depended on Richard who was fluent, although even he kept slipping into the Jersey patois, which is a mixture of a number of languages. The young girls whom I was working with would take the mickey out of my French, but I soon learned how to chat them up.

After our first week's work we had a long weekend off, as there was a public holiday on the Monday. We did have to work on the Saturday morning and the afternoon was spent clearing up our accommodation. The loft was full of straw and bales and to our amazement we found five tabby kittens, which scattered off amongst the straw bales as we appeared through the loft hatch. Two large bats were hanging from the pitched roof. Outside, there were numerous lizards basking in the sun for, despite the very cold nights, the days were still warm. The mountains that surrounded our small valley were snow-capped and each day the snowline was creeping further and further down. The Sunday we spent back in Marseille. We walked around the harbour where there were a number of cormorants basking on the decks of the many small and large yachts and fishing boats. The various Roman ruins were fascinating and the nightlife was also very interesting. It was just like Paris all over again. There were girls everywhere; some of them were very attractive but well beyond our modest pockets! We took in a film, which to my surprise was preceded by a striptease. The film itself was about striptease acts being taught at a special school. We were full of it on the way back to Les Meese and felt we had been treated to another form of 'natural science'. The next two weeks were fairly uneventful, mainly planting lettuces. The snowline on the mountains was still creeping downwards and we had a constant bitterly cold easterly wind, but the sun made it warmer in the glasshouses. One evening on returning to our room we found a green preying mantis in the doorway.

During any free time that we had we would explore the area going up in the mountains and virtually to the snowline. The mountain hares were moulting into their pure white winter coat, providing them with excellent camouflage in the snow-white terrain. One evening we stopped off for a drink in a bar in Dabisse and hanging in the corner was a dead fox. Enquiries revealed that it was a two-year-old that had been shot that morning. It was destined for a casserole, so we did not eat there!

In mid-November Monsieur Richard told us that a friend of his, who was a Paris businessman, owned a chateau about a mile away, and he wanted someone to look after it for him during the winter as he was returning to Paris. We moved in two days later. It was absolutely beautiful, standing alone about half a mile from the road along a fairly rough track. We were a little worried about the exhaust on the Mini, as it was a fairly expensive 'Twin Peaco' and quite low to the ground.

After a few teething problems, we soon settled in, although we had some difficulty getting the oil-fired Aga to light, but life was looking good. We were now planting small variegated ivy into pots. I did not want to see another lettuce plant, having planted over one hundred thousand of them.

The chateau soon warmed through and we had free run of the place. My favourite room was an artist's studio on the roof, which was all glass and gave a panoramic view of the valley and the mountains in every direction. I would just sit there and absorb the beauty. The snowline continued to creep down the mountains, and as it did so it became appreciably colder in the valley. At work we were now planting ferns in preparation for Christmas.

On Sunday, 30 November 1969, I had my first ever 'White Birthday'. The snow had finally reached the valley with a vengeance and there was a blizzard raging outside. The washing on the line had frozen solid and I can vividly remember the bed sheets swinging in the wind as stiff as board. Being Sunday, fortunately there was no work. We were a little concerned about the dilapidated garage roof and feared that the weight of the snow, combined with the gale force easterly wind, might bring it down on the car but we remained lucky. The lane to the road was deep in snow, although the snowplough had cleared the main road at the bottom. The snow was too deep to get the Mini through, so for a few days we had to walk to work. We had stocked up on supplies, so we were all right for the time being.

One morning in mid-December we were talking to Monsieur Richard about our trip so far and he informed us that there was a wild lion loose in the mountains around Grenoble and it had been there for some time. He laughed when we told him that we had slept in a tent in the mountains overlooking Grenoble! He arranged for one of the farm tractors to clear the snow off the track to the chateau. We also learned that most of the country was under snow and that we should put antifreeze in our car to protect it against minus twenty degrees Centigrade, as much colder weather was forecast. The view from the glass studio on the chateau roof was spectacular, particularly in the moonlight. The snow gave a peaceful serenity to the valley and mountains. Richard and I spent many hours talking here and discussing the future, in particular returning to Jersey. Richard had good qualifications in horticulture and I had none but I planned to rectify this when we returned to the island.

In mid-December I went down with a bad bout of flu, which laid me up for ten days. This was immediately after Richard had been off with a bad stomach. To add to our problems, Monsieur Richard had laid off a number of staff as the work was coming to an end. Although we were still working, we felt that it was only going to be a matter of time before we followed. A fleet of lorries had taken all the ivy and fern to Paris for the Christmas market and there was little demand for lettuces in this cold weather. It was snowing again and once more the lane was blocked. Walking to work was quite hard as the wind picked up the snow and blew it into our faces. The work was generally clearing up and cleaning now that the glasshouses were empty. We both knew that the job was coming to an end and it was no surprise when Monsieur Richard told us a week before Christmas that he had to let us go. That night we sat in the glass studio staring out at the white landscape and discussed what we were going to do. We knew that finding work was not going to be easy and sleeping in the car was a non-starter. As the litre of wine started to take effect, it cleared our minds and there was only one decision left – how we were going to be able to drive the thousand or so miles back to St Malo and across to Jersey. It was ironic in a way that, as we sat there making plans, we watched a large fox in the moonlit snow hunting in the fields around the chateau.

We were paid off four days before Christmas and Monsieur Richard was genuinely sorry to see us go but with the work finished he had no choice. We packed the car up and reluctantly left the chateau that had been our home for almost a month. It was with some difficulty that we managed to get the car down the track to the road, which had once again been cleared by the snowplough. We headed north back into the mountains, for although it was snowing, Monsieur Richard had advised us that the mountain route would be kept clear. We drove all day, very slowly. The scenery was spectacular, and in contrast to the barren mountain landscape of the journey down all those months ago, the scenery was now glaring white and quite beautiful.

As dusk fell, we were travelling along the side of a mountain and way down in the snow-filled valley below us was a tiny village. All the houses had their lights on, which gave it a magical appearance – a scene from a Christmas fairy tale. We eventually stopped in the small town of Roanne and checked in at a hotel for the night for the princely sum of twelve francs each. There was no way that we could have slept in the car. Roanne was just north-west of Lyon, and after breakfast we set off in a north-westerly direction. It was snowing heavily and the road was very slippery, making the front-wheel drive of the Mini a real bonus. Soon after leaving the town, a lorry in front of us jackknifed as we descended the side of a deep valley towards a small village. It seemed to broadside down the road for ever and we feared that it was going to wipe out the village. With some very skilful manoeuvring, the driver regained control and stopped. We pulled up to see if he was all right and he appreciated the gesture. Just outside the village of Lapalisse, we came across a serious accident between a lorry and a van. The road was blocked for over half an hour, and for the rest of the day we continued north-west. It took all our concentration as the conditions were atrocious and we passed numerous accidents. Just south of Châteauroux we had a puncture in the rear right-hand tyre. Changing the wheel was an endurance test, with the snow falling horizontally in the gale force easterly wind. We arrived at the town of Tours and booked into a hotel. We were both exhausted. We got the puncture repaired the following day before setting off for Le Mans, where we had a bite to eat. We eventually arrived at St Malo at 8 p.m., having driven over a thousand miles in three days in the worst conditions imaginable. We both felt physically and mentally drained. The next ferry to Jersey was in the morning, so we booked into a guest house and were given a fantastic meal as we recited our exploits of the past few days to the patron and his wife. The wine flowed as we sat in front of a huge log fire and we slept so well that night that we almost missed the ferry the next morning, which was Christmas Eve. As we sailed from St Malo and watched the French coast slowly fade in the mist and rain, I was filled with sadness. We had had a wonderful time with countless experiences that I will never forget. I read the journal that I had kept, with fond memories of the people that we had met and the wildlife we saw.

Back in Jersey I worked with Richard and his dad on the farm at the western end of the island. I was given the opportunity to attend day-release studies at the Jersey States Farm where I studied for my City & Guilds in Agriculture and Animal Husbandry. The farm included land at Le Tacq and I returned to watching the birds there when I could. Little had changed at the zoo.

Having gained my City & Guilds certificates, I returned to the mainland, where I had been offered a place at Writtle Agricultural College in Essex to continue my studies full time. Richard had decided to go to Australia, but whilst I was

in France I had decided that I should get some formal qualifications.

Whilst at Writtle, I married my first wife, Lynda, and on leaving college we moved to a farm at Tolleshunt D'Arcy on the
Essex coast, where I worked for almost a year. The wildlife
there was interesting with lots of waders on the marshes,
wildfowl in the 'Saltings' and numerous summer visitors. A
barn owl could be seen every evening hunting the deep ditch
on the land side of the sea wall.

Although I now had some reasonable qualifications in farming, I began to see no real future for me and, as a number of
fellow students on my course had joined the police force, I
followed suit in June 1973. Six weeks later our son Phillip
was born. Some years later my previous place of employment, Old Hall Farm at Tolleshunt D'Arcy, was purchased
by the RSPB and is now a major reserve for the society.

So as I moved on, another chapter of my life began.

Top: 'Nobby' the black Shetland pony.
Bottom: Female kestral.

Top: Grass snake.
Bottom: Badger cub dining.

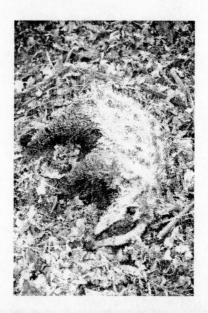

Top: Baited sow badger.
Bottom: Badger in long grass.

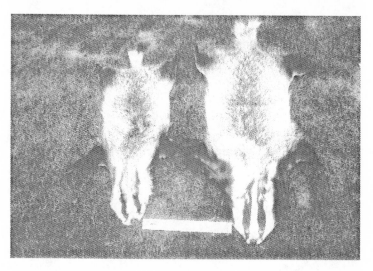

Top: 'Lucky'.
Bottom: Badger pelts (racoon?).

Top: Otter.
Bottom: Smew (Drake).

Top: A pair of fulmars.
Bottom: Wolf.

Top: Mute swan.
Bottom: Flight.

Top: Red Stag.
Bottom: The author and 'Bert'.

Wildlife and the 'Law' – My Early Years

In early June 1973, I attended Essex Police Headquarters for an interview to join the force. My previous time at the zoo and my general wildlife interests were the subject of questions by the interviewing panel, which was chaired by the assistant chief constable at the time, John Duke. I completed the interview and was accepted, subject to passing a medical. I was passed as medically fit, despite having a missing kneecap in my left knee and was sworn in that day at Chelmsford Magistrates Court.

With bags packed and not without some trepidation I set off for Eynsham Hall Police Training College at Witney, Oxford. This was the start of a thirteen-week intensive 'Law and Procedure' course, combined with marching and drill on the hall's parade square, which was situated at the front of the most imposing of buildings. It was hard work but I enjoyed it. In the mists of time one forgets the bad points and remembers only the good ones. Apart from a brief reference to the game laws in respect of poaching, there was no input on wildlife law as it stood in 1973. It was many years later that wildlife law was to take on a new perspective.

It was whilst I was at Eynsham Hall that my son Phillip was born. Due to some serious complications with Phillip and my wife Lynda, which occurred before, during and after the birth, I was given compassionate leave to be with them. Happily, both recovered, although Phil was monitored for a long time afterwards.

On leaving Eynsham Hall I was stationed at Ongar, near Epping, and it was here that I spent my two years as a probationary constable. Ongar was an excellent training ground with only two constables and a sergeant on a shift. We were kept busy. My senior constable was PC Norman 'Paddy' Rea and my first sergeant was Pete Cousins. Both were long in service and had a wealth of experience. Pete and I shared an interest in birds and he was fascinated with my tales of the zoo. Both Paddy and Pete were old-fashioned in as much as they always wore their helmets in preference to the flat caps that were primarily designed for use in the cars. I followed suit. The helmet was and still is the symbol of the traditional policeman and commands much more respect than the flat cap, even in this high-tech era of the twenty-first century.

At that time, the Ongar section covered a huge rural area on the border of the Metropolitan Police District (J & K Divisions), which ran along the southern end of Stapleford Abbotts to Abridge and beyond. Epping and Ongar Police Stations both came under Epping Forest District Council and worked closely together. It was this close liaison that saw me embroiled in my first poaching case and, as often happens in the police force, it was in at the deep end.

The incident happened during late October of that year, whilst Paddy and I were working nights and out on patrol. Around midnight we were on our way back to Ongar for a cup of tea when we were sent to the forest. We were just into the Essex ground near the Robin Hood roundabout, on the A11 trunk road into London. We met up with a forest ranger and he told us that he believed he had discovered poachers in the forest and that their van was parked at the end of a track nearby. We parked up and walked with the ranger along the dark track without torches. Fortunately, there was a full moon that was casting long shadows through the bare trees. I was quite excited and the adrenalin was pumping. This was something totally different and it beat stopping cars for having no road tax.

We reached the van and, having established that there was no one with it, the ranger opened the unlocked back door. Inside we discovered four fallow deer carcasses, all of which were does and the top one still warm. They had been disembowelled and there was a lot of blood on the floor of the van. The ranger showed us the holes in each of the animals' heads, suggesting that they had been killed with a crossbow arrow. This was confirmed when we looked at the bottom animal that had a broken shaft of a steel arrow or dart still in the back of the head. We found another hole through the chest cavity, indicating that it had taken two shots to kill this animal. Paddy immobilised the vehicle by removing the rotor arm from the engine and placing it under one of the deer carcasses.

We decided that we might need some back-up on this job, as we did not know how many poachers there were. The plan was to wait in the forest near the van and pounce on the perpetrators when they returned. Nothing would be achieved by going after them through the dark forest. Back-up duly arrived in the form of both Essex officers from Harlow and Metropolitan officers from Loughton, as we were literally on the border. The Met lads were happy for us to deal with the incident but would help in any way possible. We ended up with seven officers and two rangers. We took up positions behind trees in a semicircle around the van, staying to the side of the vehicle nearest the road. We were assuming that the poachers had gone off into the forest ahead of the van. I was thoroughly enjoying myself.

We did not have to wait long before we saw torches approaching way off through the trees. As they came nearer, we could make out four men and could hear them talking in a foreign language. The adrenalin was pumping again. As they approached the van I could see in the moonlight that they were dragging two more carcasses. These were lifted into the back of the van and one of the men climbed in with them. The rear door was shut and the three remaining men got into the front and closed their doors. It was then that we moved in on the van and the men. I should have been nervous but I was too excited. With torches blazing we reached the van. The driver was desperately trying to start the engine but it would not fire – I wonder why! The man in the back burst out through the rear door in an attempt to escape but he crashed into the arms of a huge Met PC who had the handcuffs on him before he knew what was happening. The other three gave themselves up on learning how they were outnumbered and we were met with a hurl of abuse in Greek. Of course they could not speak English but they understood the handcuffs and being put in the back of a police vehicle. They were all taken to Epping Police Station while Paddy followed in their van with its macabre load. I had seized the steel crossbow and a tube holster containing a number of nine-inch arrows some of which were bloodstained and included the other half of the broken arrow that was still in the deer in the van.

They had all learned English very quickly and by the time we reached the police station they were fluent. Each was blaming the other and all were denying using the crossbow, although it was the man in the back who had been carrying it. The crossbow was later valued at several hundreds of pounds even at 1973 prices. Each of the men gave false details at the station and it took a long time to verify who they were and where they lived. They were all subsequently charged with a number of poaching offences. The man in the back of the van had good reason to try to escape, as the Metropolitan Police also wanted him in connection with an armed robbery. The van, carcasses and crossbow were all seized as evidence and the remaining three men were released on bail. The venison was stored at a butcher's in

Ongar and the van at Harlow Police Station.

It later transpired that these four individuals were Greek Cypriots and were supplying venison to London restaurants on a big scale. They all received heavy fines at court and a destruction order was made on the crossbow. As an officer in the case, I had to give evidence in court. This was only my second experience of appearing as a witness, the first being my appearance in Jersey. The male wanted by the Met was produced at the court by the prison service, as he had been remanded in custody for trial for armed robbery. After the case, one of the group told me that what had hurt the most was losing the crossbow for which they had paid over a thousand pounds – a lot of money in those days.

That case set the pattern for my first winter in the force at Ongar. I was involved in all manner of poaching cases involving game such as pheasant, partridge, rabbit and hare. I soon developed a good knowledge of the game laws, points to prove in evidence and police powers, which were very restricted. All we could do was to seize the game along with any instruments such as nets, verify who they were and report them for the offence. This was a time-consuming exercise that one or two of my colleagues felt was rather wasted, as the fines meted out at court were paltry, pardon the pun. In spite of this I was on duty virtually every weekend either on 'earlies' (6 a.m.–2 p.m.) or 'lates' (2 p.m.–10 p.m.) dealing with poachers. They were not the traditional image of poachers – that of the old rough country boy after a bird for the pot – they were organised gangs out for profit. A brace of pheasants would fetch three to four pounds and were therefore worth taking the risk for. Although these gangs would avoid detection by hiding in ditches, hedges or by simply running away, they never offered any real violence to us; however, we did have reports of gamekeepers and landowners being set upon. Having said that, we experienced violence from some when caught and I now recall one incident when my life was threatened.

It was early one Sunday morning when Paddy and I were on an early turn. We had just finished a refreshment break and were both dealing with paperwork when we received a call from our control room. They had taken a 999 call from a local gamekeeper reporting armed poachers on his land adjacent to the railway line. The spot was between Ongar and Blake Hall – the next station down the line. Paddy and I turned out in our police Mini van and Epping dispatched a car to back us up. We met the keeper at his cottage and we all crept along a hedge leading to the line. We heard one or two shots quite nearby and once again the adrenalin was rushing. Suddenly, we reached a thin patch in the hedge and we could see the three men. They were standing next to the fence that separated the embankment from the field. Further along the fence, apparently fixed to a wooden post, was a live barn owl that appeared to be hanging on a short lead from the top of the post and was flapping frantically. We burst through the hedge and confronted the men. Two of them immediately placed their shotguns on the ground and stood still but one decided to run off across the field towards Blake Hall Railway Station. He was still carrying his side by side shotgun. Without a second thought, I gave chase, leaving Paddy and the newly arrived back-up dealing with the other two. I was running flat out across the meadow after the man who was about two hundred yards ahead of me and beginning to flag. I had him, or so I thought. Suddenly he turned around holding the gun at waist height. His stance and body language told me he was going to shoot. I hit the ground hard and put my hands over my head. Almost immediately there was a loud bang that seemed to echo round the field, followed by a second. I was okay and looked up, as I knew he would have to reload if he wanted to fire any more shots. He was running away at full speed, still carrying the gun. I got up and gave chase again.

In those days we had to carry two radio units: one receiver and one transmitter with a retractable aerial that popped up when you transmitted (if you were unlucky it went up your nose or into your eye). They were two-tone grey and very bulky. As I had hit the ground I had dropped both, so now I was on my own. The man had gained quite a distance on me but after recent events I was absolutely determined that he was not going to get away from me. Unbeknown to me, Harlow CID were carrying out observations in the car park at Blake Hall Station. There had been several thefts recently from and of vehicles parked there. On reaching the fence the man jumped over it and was immediately brought to the ground by a rugby tackle that any England forward would have been proud of. All I saw was the gun flying through the air. I reached the fence panting heavily to find that two CID officers were in the process of handcuffing the man. I remember that his nose was bleeding where he had hit the ground. The gun lay on the ground near to the group. I checked carefully that it was unloaded, it was. I handled the gun with outstretched fingers, being careful to preserve fingerprints.

The three men, who were Maltese, were taken to Harlow, where they were all charged with various firearm offences. The gentleman who had fired at me was remanded in custody due to the seriousness of the charges. CID were looking to charge him with attempted murder but he was charged with very serious firearm offence instead.

The barn owl was placed in a box, apparently none the worse for its ordeal. It was being used by the men to lure other small birds such as finches and, in this case, skylarks to the post. When birds of prey, especially nocturnal birds such as owls, appear during the day, these birds often mob them. This gave the men the opportunity to shoot the smaller birds, which are regarded as a delicacy in certain countries.

The subsequent trial of the man who had shot at me was

heard at Chelmsford Crown Court before His Honour Judge Peter Greenwood. The defendant pleaded not guilty on the basis that he had fired the gun into the air to scare me off and not to kill me. The trial lasted three days and, as the officer in the case, my evidence was last. The first day was spent on legal arguments from both defence and prosecuting councils. The second day heard evidence from the witnesses including Paddy, my colleagues who had backed us up, the gamekeeper, the CID officers and the driver of a passing train. The third day was my day, or should I say hour in the morning!

I arrived in best dress uniform feeling a little nervous as this was my first visit to Crown Court. In those days it was situated in the Old Shire Hall in the centre of Chelmsford, near Tindall Square. It was a very imposing building both from the outside and once inside. The case was being heard in Court One. I sat in the witness room with hands sweating. Eventually, the moment I was dreading arrived. I do not understand why I was so nervous as it was not me who was on trial. I stood in the witness box, which was above the rest of the courtroom but at eye level with the judge. I was sworn in. Before the prosecuting council had a chance to lead me through the evidence, the judge interrupted and said to me, 'Officer, could you satisfy the court once and for all, was the gun pointed at you or into the air?' I thought for a moment and said, 'I'm sorry, Your Honour, I am not able to answer your question truthfully as I was trying to get as low as possible in the grass.' I was looking straight at the judge who then looked at the defendant in the box with two huge prison officers either side of him. The judge looked over his half-moon glasses at the man and said, 'Quite right, quite right.' The prosecuting council then led me through my evidence but the defence council was not paying a lot of attention. He was talking to his instructing solicitor who was sitting behind him and who was in turn speaking to the defendant. After I had completed giving my evidence-in-chief, it was the defence council's opportunity to cross-examine. Before he started he asked for a brief adjournment as he wished to speak to his client. It was lunch time, so the judge adjourned until 2 p.m.

On returning, the defence council stood up and advised the judge that his client wished to change his plea to guilty. The judge looked long and hard at the defendant and asked him if that was correct. He confirmed it. The jury did not return, as they were no longer required. The judge was most unhappy that the court's time had been wasted and said so in no uncertain terms. He adjourned the court for four weeks for sentencing, pending reports from the probation service. I was in court, off duty, for the sentencing when the judge informed the defendant that he considered this matter to be very serious and the sentence would reflect his view of the offence. He was given eight years in prison. I was astonished, as I had thought he might receive a one-year sentence.

To conclude this story, the barn owl went to a bird sanctuary where she successfully bred the following year raising four beautiful owlets.

After that case, which received a lot of media coverage, my reputation throughout the Harlow Division and the force grew. A number of wildlife matters started to come my way, bearing in mind of course that this was sixteen years before police wildlife liaison officers were even in their embryonic stage. Poaching offences were still our main workload on Sundays. We went through a period of poaching on the railway embankment between Ongar and Epping, where the branch line ended. The embankment was full of large rabbit warrens and a popular area for the poachers. They were either foolhardy or mad, for they would regularly cross the electrified line from one embankment to another with apparent disregard to the extreme danger they were placing themselves in. Obviously the British Transport

Police covered the line and the embankment on either side but the poachers did not just stick to the railway property, and that was where we came in. We would deal with them and obtain statements from London Underground, stating that no one was allowed to take rabbits or game from their property and from gamekeepers who could see them clearly ferreting along the embankments.

One particular incident always comes to mind; it involved four men who were working the line from Blake Hall to Ongar with nets and ferrets. I was on my own on patrol in the Mini van when I received a radio message from our control. They had taken a 999 call from the stationmaster at Epping Underground Station who had been informed by a train driver that there was a gang of men on the line. As I approached Blake Hall Station, I suddenly spotted the men on the embankment. They were unaware of my presence. I parked the van behind a hedge out of sight and watched them through binoculars. They were placing 'purse' nets over the rabbit warren and then putting ferrets down the holes. They appeared to be catching a lot of rabbits. A gamekeeper and the officer from North Weald joined me. The men on the line had come over the fence off the embankment into a small coppice. As soon as they were out of sight, we made our move.

We entered the coppice from the other end and halfway through I heard a shout from some way ahead of us, followed by men running through the undergrowth. We gave chase and, on reaching the far end of the coppice, we saw the men climbing over the wire fence on to the embankment. When they saw us they ran off up the slope and on to the line without any regard for their own safety. A high-voltage electrified line was below their feet and they ran across it. We stopped at the line – there was no way that we were going to endanger our lives. We called up on the radio for assistance and the men were eventually intercepted on returning to their van that was parked up a track near the embankment, further along towards Ongar. Ironically, they were in more trouble for trespassing on railway land than for the poaching. They all received heavy fines in court.

On another occasion we were up on the railway line, or I should say by the side of it, chasing three men who were running along the same side as us. They were not prepared to risk electrocution. Suddenly, all three disappeared leaving their dogs wandering aimlessly around the embankment and across the track. I knew that there was a culvert that passed under the track in the area that they had disappeared. As we got nearer, my colleague Paddy had an idea. We managed to catch the dogs that still had their leads attached. As we approached the culvert, Paddy shouted in his broad Irish accent, 'Leave the dogs on the track. There's a train coming that will kill them.' There was no train in sight and we had the dogs safely beside us. Almost immediately the three men appeared from the culvert shouting, 'All right, guv'nor, were coming.' The bluff had worked. While Paddy spoke to them I climbed down the steep descent to the culvert. In it I found a small box with two ferrets, nets, pegs and a canvas bag containing thirty-six rabbits. Heavy fines were again meted out for being on railway property.

On one occasion I almost lost the evidence. It was early one Sunday and I was out on my own as Paddy was on leave. I was sent to see to poachers on land at Stapleford Abbotts. With the help of the local gamekeeper I managed to catch the poachers red-handed. They were in possession of two ferrets in a wooden box with a wire front, nets, pegs and two dead rabbits. They had only just started. I placed the rabbits and the ferrets in the back of the police Mini van and spoke to the three men. It took me ages to process all three, bearing in mind that this was long before the days of the police national computer. As all three men were from London, and it took quite a while to verify their addresses with the

Metropolitan Police. Eventually, once I was satisfied that they had given their correct names and addresses, they were reported. At that time the law only permitted me to take possession of the rabbits and nets as evidence. I opened the back of the van to return the ferrets and an unbelievable sight greeted me. The hungry ferrets had gnawed a hole out of the box and had virtually devoured the rabbits. Only the feet remained, which was just as well as that was all we needed to produce in court as evidence. Had the rabbits been completely devoured, I might well have had some difficulties in court.

Another story begins one morning when Paddy and I, having just finished our refreshment break, were sent to poachers at High Ongar. On our arrival we found the landowner with two men at a warren. There were signs that the men had been digging at the entrance and it soon transpired why. They had put a Jack Russell terrier down the hole to flush out rabbits – a common alternative to ferrets. Unfortunately, the terrier had become stuck in the warren. We could hear it whimpering from deep in the ground. The landowner agreed for the men to dig the terrier out and we would deal with the question of poaching afterwards. Paddy and I were both concerned for the welfare of the dog. It soon became apparent that the dog, whose name was Banjo, was a lot deeper than was first thought and we all ended up taking a turn at digging. It was hard work in wet heavy clay and we were all plastered after four hours of hard slog. We had made a huge hole but the dog was still a long way away. Paddy decided to enlist the help of the local fire brigade and the tender from Ongar turned out. With fresh diggers and more hands we had reached Banjo within an hour. He appeared to have fallen down a four-foot hole deep within the warren and had been unable to climb out. One of the firemen reached down into the hole and lifted the terrier free, much to the relief of everyone. Banjo did not appear to be unduly stressed by his experience and greeted his master with excited licks as he held him – typical terrier. The entire operation had taken almost six hours and the landowner felt that the men had suffered enough and decided not to press charges for poaching. Paddy and I were late off duty that day. Our uniforms had to go for cleaning and Banjo's story appeared in the local press.

In addition to rabbit and pheasant poaching, we also experienced an increase in hare coursing, which was covered by the same act and section as other poaching, namely 'Trespassing in pursuit of game'. Men with greyhounds would regularly visit the area, often training their dogs for the White City and Walthamstow stadiums. Alternatively, they would bet there and then in the field on the outcome of the course. The aim was not necessarily to kill the hare but to see how many times the hounds could make it turn, or to see who could get the closest to it before they ran out of steam. Upon being caught, the favourite reply when asked what they were doing in the fields lined up with their hounds was, 'We're only walking our dogs, guv'nor.' This mainly occurred at weekends through the winter when the fields had either no crops or very short crops, enabling the hounds to see the hares quite easily. Greyhounds and long dogs hunt primarily by sight. These cases were in addition to main line policing such as dealing with road accidents, burglaries, thefts and general enquiries. Hare coursing was to play a major part of my policing career much later in my service.

Moving away from the numerous poaching incidents that dominated my early police career, I also became involved with a number of other wildlife matters. A complaint was received at Epping that a young boy was shooting birds in his garden with an air rifle, mainly during the weekend. Inevitably the matter was passed to me to investigate.

Reluctantly I was given two weekends to keep observations from the neighbour's house.

The garden where the youth lived was overgrown and very untidy. Nettles and thistles abounded. There was a bird table close to the house and it was here that he was allegedly shooting the birds. The first weekend I arrived at the neighbour's house at 6 a.m. under the cover of darkness and sat in the bedroom overlooking the garden. Needless to say, nothing happened on the Saturday or the Sunday. Similarly, the following Saturday was fruitless as it poured with rain all day. On the Sunday, the last day of the operation, I arrived early. A lovely couple who kept me plied with tea and sandwiches owned the house I was using. On that Sunday they treated me to a full fried breakfast and I thought, This is the life. At about 11 a.m. I saw the youth placing bread on the bird table, and shortly afterwards a blackbird came down to investigate. Before it was able to eat anything, there was a crack and the poor bird was dead on the ground below the table. Shortly afterwards I saw a goldfinch feeding on a thistle seed head further down the garden. Once again a loud crack rang out and the beautiful bird fell from the seed head into the dense undergrowth beneath.

I had seen enough. I rushed around and banged on the door, which was answered by the youth. He initially denied everything but once he realised that I had been watching, his arrogance evaporated and he admitted everything. I seized the air rifle, which was a .22, along with the ammunition to go with it. I also recovered the two dead birds that still lay where they had fallen. He subsequently appeared at Epping Magistrates Court, where he received a heavy fine and the court ordered the destruction of the weapon and ammunition. The time spent on the operation was vindicated by the good public relations, generated from the subsequent press articles.

Away from prosecution, another amusing incident occurred one night while I was out on patrol with one of the Ongar special constables, Sid Southgate. It was about 11 p.m. and we were patrolling through Stapleford Abbotts when I spotted a rook on the side of the road. As we approached, it did not move and it was obvious that it was injured. I stopped the car and got out. I approached the bird and picked it up. On examination in the headlights of the police car I could see no obvious injuries, so I placed it in the floor of the car and we continued our patrol. I intended to take it back to the police station at midnight – our tea break time.

About half and hour after picking up the bird, we were on our way back to Ongar when we received a call asking us to attend a road accident, ironically back at Stapleford Abbotts. On our arrival we found one car in a ditch having collided with a tree; the driver was staggering around in the road. I asked him if he was all right and, when he replied, the tell-tale smell of alcohol emanated on his breath. Sid placed him in the back of the car while I checked the smashed up car for any more casualties – there were none. I breathalysed the driver and it turned the crystals in the tube bright green. He was arrested. On our way back to the station the man fell asleep in the back, sitting bolt upright. Sid and I were talking when suddenly there was a loud fluttering of wings in the back and I remembered the rook. I looked in the rear-view mirror only to see the man fully awake and wide eyes staring at the rook that was sitting on his lap. Sid and I were in hysterics (oh, for a camera!). We later related the story to the sergeant who initially thought that we had been drinking as well until we showed him the bird. His comment was, 'How are you going to explain that in court if this driver tells the magistrates that whilst in the back of a police car a rook landed in his lap?' My answer was, 'If he does then they will think he was even more drunk than he actually was.' At the subsequent hearing the driver did not mention the bird!

One Boxing Day I was on late turn (2 p.m.–10 p.m.) and out on patrol on my own in narrow country lanes of Stapleford Tawney when I came across what appeared to be a dead rabbit. At this time I was rearing an injured owl back to full health and a dead rabbit would last it some days. I got out, and as I approached the rabbit I became aware that something was wrapped around it. As I got close to it I realised that it was a stoat and that it had the rabbit by the throat. I touched the rabbit thinking that the stoat would let go and run off but it did not. I was determined to get the rabbit and went back to the car for a shovel intending to remove the stoat. As I returned to the rabbit, the stoat ran off into the undergrowth, so I picked up the rabbit and placed it in the passenger footwell of the car. Just as I got back in and shut the door, the stoat reappeared looking most indignant as it sat bolt upright looking at me. I watched, fascinated, as it smelt around for the rabbit, slowly working its way towards the police car. (If only I had had a camera.) I left the engine turned off, and it seemed to me that the stoat knew that the rabbit was in the car. It was running around outside, occasionally sitting up. On one occasion it sat up outside my door and we stared at each other. At that moment I had a call on the radio and needed to turn around for a job in the opposite direction. I started the engine and the stoat scuttled off. I drove off up the road, turned around in a field gateway and back down the road again only to be confronted by the stoat sitting up in the middle of the road looking right at me. I had to slow down as I approached and the aggrieved predator did not move until the very last moment. I felt a little sorry for the stoat but the owl's welfare was paramount to me. I have never experienced anything like that since.

During my early service at Ongar I developed a sound knowledge of game law, which was to hold me in good stead for the remainder of my service. I became renowned for my wildlife interests and was known as the 'Poaching King' by my colleagues. After two very happy years at Ongar I decided that I wanted to become a village policeman, and after a couple of unlucky applications for local beats I was eventually successful. My first wife, Lyn, our son, Phillip, and myself moved to Thaxted, where I took up the position of the 'local bobby'. We soon settled in. My appointment was announced in the local press and my wildlife interests and work at Jersey Zoo became a major feature. I joined the local executive of Essex Wildlife Trust and a number of other wildlife organisations.

Within weeks of the move I became embroiled in my first hare-coursing incident. It was a good case as I actually saw them coming across a large field on the outskirts of Thaxted. Normally it is either the landowner or gamekeeper who first sees the coursing and obtains evidence before calling in the police, but this time I had caught them red-handed. They were not at all happy when I intercepted them at their van. My reputation soon spread through the local farming community.

During my early days at Thaxted I also became involved in policing hunts. We regularly had foxhunts on a Wednesday and Saturday. The main role of the police at hunts is to prevent a breach of the peace by either the protestors, known as 'Sabs' or 'Antis', or members of the hunt or their followers. Feelings would run high in both parties. Quiet, rational, mild-mannered people would turn into ranting, raving, irrational antagonists – and that applied to both sides. With emotions so electrified, confrontations were almost inevitable. This was particularly so with the Saturday hunts when gangs of fifty plus sabs would descend on a hunt and chaos would reign. In the early days we were virtually powerless, particularly if the sabs wandered on to the fields and woods where the hunt was in progress. Trespass in this form at that time was a civil matter and the police could not get involved. However, the law has now changed, giving police more powers to deal with problems of trespass in this form. As police officers, we had to remain impartial, irrespective of our own views. A lot of police resources were committed to the Saturday hunts by Essex Police – a great deal more than most of the neighbouring forces – but it remained force policy that we would police hunts to allow them to go about their lawful business. A lot of public order problems were experienced by Essex hunts, hence the police presence.

On the Wednesday hunts, my dear friend and member of

the special constabulary, Dave Kinnley, often joined me. He was a ranking officer within the specials, holding the equivalent rank to chief inspector in the regulars. He had served in the specials for over twenty years when I moved to Thaxted, where he had lived all his life. He worked in a local shop and as Wednesday was 'half-day closing' he would accompany me for the day. He loved being out in the country and we soon became very close friends. He was a giant of a man in every aspect, at six foot four inches tall he towered over me at six foot. He weighed twenty-two stone and I always wondered how he managed to get into my police Mini van – my first vehicle when I arrived at Thaxted. The Wednesday hunts were normally fairly peaceful; one or two sabs would sometimes turn up but being outnumbered by about twenty to one, they were generally quiet. We would have one Wednesday hunt a month during the season, and if Dave had a Saturday off, which he often tried to do when there was a hunt on, he would join me then as well.

On Saturday hunts the sabs would normally arrive at the meet itself in a convoy of vans. The meet, as the title suggests, is where all the horses and riders, known as 'the field', would meet and where the hounds led by 'the whipper in' would join the field. After a stirrup cup of something warming – hunting in mid-winter can be a cold affair – the hunt would ride off, often through the sabs with a lot of shouting and horn blowing. This usually occurred on the road and we would have to clear a path. This was where Dave's size came in handy – few people argued with him and I hid behind him!

At one Saturday hunt Dave was with me. There was a field of about forty horses and about the same number of antis, who were relatively quiet for a change. One of the joint masters, however, was deliberately trying to taunt the antis to the point where I had to intervene. I warned him that his conduct and not that of the antis was likely to cause a breach of the peace and he would render himself liable to being arrested. He muttered something unrepeatable and continued taunting the antis right in front of me, totally ignoring the warning. Dave and I approached his horse. Dave took the reins and I said those immortal words, 'I have given you a warning which you have chosen to ignore. I am now arresting you for conduct likely to cause a breach of the peace.' While I cautioned him, he came out with the classic reply, 'You can't do that.' (Those are the wrong words to say to a police officer!) He was off his horse quicker than he had mounted it, despite loud protests from the other huntsmen and women who had gathered round in a very menacing circle. His horse was handed to one of the whippers in and I conveyed him to the local police station, where he was detained until the end of the hunt. The resulting formal complaint was served on me but was later withdrawn. The complaint was for 'Unlawful Arrest' but the arrest was perfectly justified and my actions vindicated by a very senior Essex police officer.

Conversely, the antis or sabs were not above being arrested if they overstepped the mark. The typical scenario was for them to blow a hunting horn to draw the hounds away from the huntsmen particularly the whipper in. I must say that some of the sabs were quite accomplished at this! While this was going on, others would be running along the hedges and through the woods that were about to be hunted with 'Anti Mate' spray to interfere with the hound's scenting. Warnings were given and ignored and then arrests would be made. On one occasion a sab blew his horn in an attempt to draw the hounds across a busy main road. He ignored my warning and spent the rest of the day courtesy of Essex Police. Fortunately, the hounds did not cross the road, as there would have been a massacre.

In 1993, the force commenced filming hunts with video

cameras, using specially trained officers. I was one of the first trained. Each cameraman had a minder and the primary role of the pair was to gain evidence on film of the activities of the sabs and the hunt. These officers were known as 'Evidence Gatherers'. The filmed evidence was very useful in court to give the judiciary some idea of the scale of the public order problems at some hunts. The hunts and the sabs were not to be outdone and they started their own filming of each other and the police.

At the time of writing this chapter in my life, I have been covering hunt meetings for almost twenty-seven years, and over that time I have gathered many stories, some humorous, some tragic – enough in fact for a book on its own. The following are a few that readily come to mind.

One incident occurred when Dave and I were covering a Wednesday meet at Great Sampford, just outside Thaxted. It was November and it was a cold but bright and sunny day. The huntsmen looked resplendent in their 'Pinks'. As the horses exhaled, their breath condensed and hung in the air. The hounds were excited as they left their box. The whipper in brought them together and off they went. There were no sabs but one local resident objected quite vociferously at being held up on the road while the hunt moved off and at the mess on the road. She did not appreciate Dave's comment that 'It's good for your roses, Madam'. The remainder of the early morning proved uneventful as the field sat at a number of spots whilst the hounds drew various covers without success. The hounds then entered a large wood on the outskirts of the village. The field stood some way off and waited. Dave and I were sitting in the police Mini van on the road about two hundred yards from the wood, which ran parallel to the road. After what seemed like an age, the hounds came out of the wood close to where the hunt master and the field were sitting. It was obvious that they had not found a fox or any scent. There appeared to be some discussions as to where they were going next, with much pointing of fingers. As the hounds started to move away from us with the hunt following, Dave suddenly pointed to a spot not fifty yards along the side of the wood from where the hunt had been waiting. There in the bright sunlight was a huge fox that had stepped out of the wood, apparently unperturbed by what was going on. It shook itself and then started to approach us across the field along the line of a ditch. What a sight that was – the hunt riding off in one direction and the fox sauntering off in the other. Dave and I were totally spellbound and it would have made a wonderful photograph.

The fox stopped about twenty-five yards from where we were standing. I can only assume that our forms were lost to the fox as we had a tree behind us. It sniffed the air and then sat on its haunches and appeared to look back at the disappearing hunt. We had both carefully got out of the van to watch the spectacle. The fox appeared to be unaware of our presence or that of the hunt, which by now was almost out of sight. Eventually, the fox got to its feet and sauntered slowly back to the wood, its coat shining in the sunlight. It selected a point along the side of the wood and hopped in, disappearing from our view. Dave was in hysterics. Neither of us had seen anything similar to that before and it was one of those really magical moments that neither of us would ever forget.

One Saturday hunt I was the chauffeur for the silver commander for the hunt, Inspector Martin Reed, in a big four-wheel drive Land Rover Discovery. It was a bright sunny January morning and, with no sabs, it had the makings of a relatively quiet day – famous last words. Soon after the hunt rode off, a fox ran out of a dense bramble hedge and the chase was on. However, it was short-lived, as the fox ran up a drainage pipe. It was confrontation time. Hunt monitors from the League Against Cruel Sports, who just happened to live nearby and who saw the fox enter the pipe, began to argue with the hunt's terrier man. He had put a terrier up the pipe to flush the fox out in order to continue the chase. To complicate the issue even further, members of the local Badger Protection Group were present and were alleging that there was a badger in the pipe, using it as a temporary sett. This would mean that it was legally protected and the placing of a terrier in the pipe would constitute an offence under the act if the terrier man knew that there was a badger in there. Verbal chaos then ensued with Martin Reed and other police officers trying to calm the situation down.

While all this was going on, I managed to slip away unnoticed. I walked up the track, following the line of the pipe. Eventually, around a corner and out of sight behind a hedge I found an inspection cover for the pipe. Checking that no one was looking, I tried to lift the cover, which initially would not move. After a lot of effort it finally came up and the sight that greeted me was quite remarkable. No badger to be seen but a fox was cowering in a corner of the square chamber with pipes leading in and out. In the opposite corner the head of the terrier was just emerging. Out of the three of us I don't know who was more surprised. Without a thought for my own safety, I stepped into the chamber, still holding the cover up, and blocked off the exit of the terrier. I beckoned the fox out, which I believe was a vixen. She needed no encouragement. As she leapt out of the chamber, her brush lifted in the breeze as she disappeared through a hedge and away. I replaced the chamber cover just as the terrier entered it yapping excitedly. I wandered back to the melee at the end of the pipe but only Martin had noticed my absence. The terrier man was trying to retrieve his dog, which eventually appeared, but he was mystified as to how the dog had not flushed the fox. The hunt moved off, followed by a very confused terrier man. As we drove off Martin was quiet but eventually broke his silence and asked,

'Did you let that fox out somehow?' The question took me a little by surprise as we drove down the lane and I had to think quickly of a safe answer. Out of the corner of my eye I could see that he had a big smile on his face. I smiled back and said, 'Of course not, sir.' He said, 'You're a liar, but well done anyway!' For weeks afterwards the terrier man spoke of the fox that simply vanished up a pipe!

Another memorable incident involved a fox and two hounds, and was one of those magical moments I keep telling people about. It was a beautiful day after a misty start during a Saturday hunt, just before Christmas. It was comparatively warm for the time of year and I was out with a colleague, who like myself had covered hunts for many years. We were in a Land Rover Discovery parked up in a field, which overlooked a valley. There was a wood on the other side, which the hounds were drawing through. On this day there were no sabs and we were enjoying the spectacle. The hunt was about one hundred and fifty yards from where we were sitting. Between us there was a low hedge, which ran parallel to the valley. We were just remarking that it was a lovely day when suddenly a beautiful fox sauntered through the hedge and trotted casually towards us without an apparent care in the world. The windows were open on our vehicle, so we switched off the radio and watched intently. The fox looked like a dog from its form and shape of head and was resplendent as the sun caught its magnificent red winter coat. It stopped about fifteen feet from us and looked at us with ears pressed forward for well over a minute, before trotting off around our vehicle and eventually disappearing into a bramble thicket behind us.

That was truly a wonderful sight in itself, but there was more to come. We were remarking on the beautiful creature when two hounds came through the hedge where the fox had appeared. Their noses were to the ground and it was obvious that they were on the fox's scent. Then something quite remarkable happened – something that neither of us had witnessed before in all our years of policing hunts. The two hounds moved away from the hedge, then stopped. The rest of the pack was way off in the distance, running around in circles in the field trying to pick up any scent. In hunting terms this is called 'casting'. The two hounds stopped not far from us and faced each other sitting on their haunches with their front legs straight. They looked like a pair of bookends. As if by some pre-arranged signal, they both looked straight up at the sky and gave out a quite awesome and eerie howl, which seemed to reverberate across the valley and through the bare trees. They repeated this three or four times, their breath condensing in the air and seeming to hang over the hounds. The air was still. We were transfixed by the moment. (Oh, for a camera!) The rest of the hounds heard these howls and, moments later, bounded through the hedge at various points and gathered round the two 'bookends' that were still sitting. When the last hound had burst through the hedge, they got up, greeted some of their colleagues and then with noses to the ground they led the pack away on the fox's scent. The bramble was too dense for them, so they appeared to pass through the hedge on either side of it and out of sight. We were absolutely speechless as we moved off to follow. The huntsmen as usual were way behind. The fox had made good ground and the pack soon lost the trail, despite casting for some time. Eventually, the whipper in called the hounds in and they all went off to draw another wood. There was something quite primeval about what we had witnessed: the howl that these two hounds had given out was like nothing that either of us had heard before and was quite spine-chilling. We spoke about it for months afterwards.

Not all hunts were as peaceful as those previously described. Soon after I became an evidence gatherer at hunt meetings, we had a major incident at a Saturday hunt that became known as 'The Siege of Stagdon Cross'. The hunt was just moving off when we were hit by approximately two hundred saboteurs who had apparently appeared from nowhere. We were vastly outnumbered and we became pinned down in a farmyard with the hunt. Fighting broke out between the rival factions, which I tried to film by standing on the back of the police Discovery vehicle. However, it soon became apparent that my minder and I were well away from any police back-up – what little of it there was in the early stages – so we decided to beat a hasty retreat to the relative safety of the vehicle. I continued filming but my view was very poor. Eventually the back-up arrived, including a contingent from the Metropolitan Police, but by this time the hunt had decided to call it a day. I believe that at least two huntsmen had been injured and a number of police officers had also needed hospital treatment, although none were seriously hurt. This was probably the most serious and potentially volatile hunting incident that I have been involved in to date and it became legendary in police and hunting circles. The sabs who arrived this day were not the regular ones. It later transpired that many were members of the 'Anti Police League', who had used this hunt meeting to have a go at Essex Police and knew nothing about hunting. The force learned a few lessons the hard way that day.

The end of season hunt was normally held towards the end of March each year and usually resulted in a few problems as manpower levels to cover the meeting are generally raised. However, I recall one occasion when I was covering an end-of-season hunt as acting sergeant. Resources had been made available to cover the hunt, but they had been held on standby at police stations all over the county. I was deployed to the hunt meet at a remote farm within the Dunmow Police section. It was a lovely day and everything was going along nicely until chaos set in as the farm was effectively blocked off by over one hundred sabs who had arrived from nowhere. They had managed to slip past the police spotters who had been strategically placed throughout the county. The situation was reminiscent of Stagdon Cross – one lone police Discovery at one end of the farmyard with the hunt behind and one hundred sabs in front, intent on preventing the hunt from moving off. The only way out was across the yard. I was representing the police along with a very young, nervous probationer who was turning paler by the minute. Fortunately, many of the sabs I recognised from previous meetings, so I went over to them and asked them to move off the private property back to the public road at the end of the lane. To my utter amazement they agreed. I was expecting a hail of abuse, but they left the yard and ran back to the road. The hunt then moved off across the yard and out of the farm via the rear. It then became apparent why the sabs had agreed to leave so readily. They had moved along the road and then ran en masse across the field towards the hunt. There was little I could do to prevent it but fortunately the hunt had the turn of speed to leave the sabs behind. There was the pungent smell of 'Anti Mate' in the air and the sound of a hunting horn that was not coming from the hunt.

As soon as the sabs had arrived, I had called for urgent back-up but the first police unit to arrive was the helicopter, which was there purely to monitor and assess the situation. Eventually, the back-up did arrive but there had already been several confrontations between individual sabs, huntsmen and hunt followers. Allegations were flying in all directions, and amongst this I was contacted by the duty inspector some twenty miles away, who instructed me to inform the hunt master that we could not guarantee the safety of the hunt and therefore the police suggested that they pack up. This did not go down at all well for the hunt felt that the sabs had won the day and prevented the hunt from going about its lawful business. Initially, the hunt refused to pack up but after one or two missiles from the sabs hit home, it was decided to finish. By the time the main back-up had arrived, the horses were being loaded into their boxes, amidst cheers from the sabs. The front page of the local paper the following week featured the incident and the hunt chairman had this to say about the police in the article: 'ESSEX POLICE WERE SHOWN TO BE WEAK AND LEADERLESS.' This did not go down at all well with the divisional commander, who had a meeting with the hunt chairman. He, I believe, was left in no uncertain terms regarding the policing of that or any other hunt. For my part I had to spend two days preparing a duty report on the entire incident, as the hunt chairman had made a formal complaint to the assistant chief constable. I pointed out that there were no assaults reported and no damage reported by either party.

Before I leave hunting, I must recount one final incident involving a hunt meeting on the coastal side of Essex that I was asked to advise on. I was off duty at home, with my feet up in front of a lovely log fire, enjoying a beer, when the phone rang at about 3 p.m. It was the duty inspector at this particular hunt who had a problem he needed urgent advice on. A fox was believed to have run into a pipe in a ditch and a terrier had been put up the pipe to flush it out (sounds familiar?). On this occasion, however, the terrier had come back out of the pipe with a bloodied nose. A torch up the pipe revealed a badger, and it was thought that there was a cub with it. Members of the local badger group were making all manner of allegations against the terrier man for interfering with a badger sett. The inspector was not too familiar with the badger act and, therefore, to defuse the situation, the terrier man was invited to attend the local police station to sort the matter out. Hence the phone call. The situation was further complicated as the badger group wanted to smash the twenty-foot long pipe to get the badger out as it was believed to be injured, although the light from the torch had not shown any injuries. A police officer was left on guard at the pipe.

It was an interesting situation and one that I had come across before. The advice I gave the inspector was that the terrier man would not commit an offence if he genuinely believed that there was a fox and not a badger in the pipe. As I pointed out to the hapless inspector, no terrier man in his right mind would put his dog in a pipe knowing that there was a badger in there. They are formidable creatures, as a future chapter will show. On the second point with regards to smashing the pipe, there would be no justification in the law for doing that. It was obvious that the sow badger had adopted the pipe as a nursery sett, and even if she had been injured, the course of action would likely terrify her and so it could not be justified. Badgers will recover naturally from the most horrendous injuries. The inspector was very grateful. A few days later I did check with the National Federation of Badger Groups, who endorsed my advice. Badgers do feature very highly in my work, primarily due to the level of protection that they enjoy, and for this reason I have devoted an entire chapter to them.

I have many more hunting stories that I could relate but I believe that the previous few will give the reader some idea of the complex issues that arise on this most emotive of subjects. Little mild-mannered old ladies who have probably never spoken to a police officer in their lives turn into ranting, raving, hysterical, irrational agents provocateurs, whilst we must remain impartial.

Soon after we moved to Thaxted, I quickly became known for my wildlife interests and I was contacted on all manner of aspects of natural history. I was appointed as the first warden for a small nature reserve acquired by the Essex Wildlife

Trust on the outskirts of Thaxted. This is known as Sweetings Meadow. At one and a half acres it is one of the smallest of the eighty plus reserves that the trust own, but it is vitally important as it is prized for its wild orchids, in particular the bee orchid, common spotted and pyramidal orchids.

I was also asked to write articles in local newspapers on wildlife issues of interest and other local publications. One of the spin-offs from these was that I began to receive requests to give talks to local groups and organisations on wildlife, using my own slides. Much later these talks were to feature more prominently in my life.

One or two injured animals and birds began to arrive on the doorstep of the police house, particularly in the spring when fledglings, mainly starlings, sparrows and blackbirds, would be brought to me by some kind, well-meaning child. On virtually every occasion I would suggest that they returned it to wherever it was found, to enable its parents to look after the hapless bird. Even tawny owlets would arrive, but the advice was the same.

At one Wednesday hunt, I was with Dave when a local farmer approached us with a box containing an injured kestrel that was unable to fly. We brought the beautiful bird home and arranged for it to be examined by a local veterinary friend of mine. He confirmed that the bird had fractured its sternum and also stated that it had a fifty–fifty chance of survival. The odds were the same as to whether it would fly again. Despite its condition, the bird was quite lively and I decided to have an attempt at rearing it back to full health. The first few days were fairly critical, as stress will normally kill a bird.

It was mid-winter, so we kept it indoors and it began to take morsels of food, particularly slivers of raw chicken breast. After a week it became apparent that the bird would survive, so I contacted the Department of the Environment to register it as temporarily disabled. The bird had arrived in mid-February, and as the days warmed up, I built an aviary in the back garden, where it happily sat on a perch. Fed on mice, shrews and even morsels of rabbit, it thrived, and after a few weeks it began to open its wings. It was almost three months before it could fly properly again and I hacked it back to the wild at the end of May. We regularly saw it afterwards, hovering over some open waste ground behind the house. During its convalescence it had lost one of its tail feathers, which made it quite identifiable when hovering with its tail fanned out. It was a lovely feeling to see this most magnificent of birds flying freely again after being confined for so long.

The baby hedgehog was another creature that regularly arrived on our doorstep. We would feed them up for a few days and then release them on the same waste ground that the kestrel patrolled. He was no threat to them.

In the late 1970s two of the villages within my beat began to suffer from the activities of an arsonist whose speciality was burning down thatched houses. A major police operation was set up to catch him and part of this operation was to interview every resident in the two villages with a questionnaire over the course of one weekend. It was a large-scale operation involving forty officers calling at every house, some of which were widely dispersed. On the Saturday morning I was out with the local chief inspector, who was a tall, well-dressed man, who always had an immaculate uniform and shoes that you could see your face in. The creases in his trousers could cut you and there was never a speck of dust or hair on his uniform.

Our task was to visit some of the more remote farms in the area and we had been taking it in turns. We drove up to one particular farmhouse, which I knew well. The boss said that he would do this one and got out of the car armed with his clipboard complete with questionnaire. As he was about to shut the door I said to him, 'Watch the geese, sir,' and he replied with a dismissive, 'Yes, yes.' He adjusted his hat and strode up the drive to the house. The main door was around the back and I had mentioned this to him. He disappeared around the corner and seconds later I heard an almighty cacophony coming from the side of the house. Suddenly, the questionnaires were drifting towards the police vehicle on the stiff breeze. I got out and ran around the side of the house. The sight that greeted me would have been worth a photograph. The chief inspector was on the ground trying to get to his feet whilst still being attacked by about a dozen white geese. He was covered from head to foot in goose muck, to put it politely. I managed to get the geese away and helped him to his feet. In doing so, I managed to receive a handful of goose muck myself. Even the boss's hat was covered and he grabbed this and his clipboard and stormed off back to the car. I followed behind trying desperately not to laugh, as his back was filthy. The geese followed us with necks parallel to the ground, hissing and honking. On reaching the car I grabbed a plastic bin bag out of the back (used for picking up badger road casualties) and covered the seat with it before he got in. As I did so he said, 'Why didn't you tell me that those... things were there?' I retorted, 'I did, sir. As you got out, I warned you about the geese.' He made no reply. Needless to say, there was no one in at the house anyway. I took the chief inspector back to Saffron Walden Police Station, where I left him. He did not come out with me again during that operation (I can't think why).

For my first ten years at Thaxted, life ticked over. I had long periods of acting sergeant duties at both Saffron Walden and Dunmow. In 1984, the beginning of one of the biggest police operations that Britain was likely to see took place, as the

National Union of Miners staged industrial action that was to continue for over a year, with the pits in Nottinghamshire defying the strike. This was a national police operation with officers from all over the country being deployed. I spent a total of twelve weeks on the dispute, with odd weeks throughout the strike. I carried out duties in Nottinghamshire, Leicestershire and South Yorkshire, and the flora and fauna were quite fascinating. One of the many things that struck me was the number of skylarks in the region, but I was told that the grassed-over slag heaps provided excellent nesting and feeding sites. Clumber Forest in Nottingham appeared to be full of green woodpeckers and it was here that I saw my first pied flycatcher. We spent one week on night duty on a roundabout along the A1 at Newark. We saw numerous nocturnal creatures including foxes, owls and even a barn owl. But the highlight for all the ten lads on our crew bus was a badger that trotted past us one night, totally unperturbed by our presence. It was the talking point for the remainder of the week. Bats of various sizes would often fly through our headlights and torch beams. These were mainly pipistrelle and long-eared bats, as they caught winged insects on the warm, sultry summer nights. It was interesting to compare the wildlife of the Midlands with that of the South-East. The dispute was one that I do not believe anyone who was involved in it will ever forget.

Soon after the miners' dispute finished, I became embroiled in an incident with a local farmer and a huge well-established badger sett on his ground. I was contacted one Easter by a colleague on the Essex Wildlife Trust local executive, who had discovered snares around this sett. We trudged across the fields. It was bright and sunny but there was a covering of snow that had appeared overnight. The sett was on a wooded bank with a stream at the base. We found a total of ten snares around some of the sett entrances. We photographed them in situ and then removed them. I subsequently prosecuted the farmer for attempting to take/kill badgers and for using self-locking snares which are illegal. At the subsequent trial we lost the case on a couple of technicalities. A lot of lessons were learned on that case.

An amusing incident occurred at Thaxted Church one year. Dave and I were on duty at the church during a Thaxted Festival concert. A military band from a local army barracks were playing and *we* were the security! The band concluded their performance at the end of the evening with Tchaikovsky's 1812 Overture. We were seated behind the band and out of sight of the thousand-strong audience but we had a good view. Towards the end of the performance Dave leaned across to me and whispered, 'You watch what happens when it comes to the cannon fire.' I was unsure of what he meant but did not query it. Almost immediately afterwards a dozen soldiers appeared from behind us and lined up with rifles behind the band, immediately in front of us. We stood up to watch and I covered my ears. Suddenly, there was an enormous bang to simulate the canon fire in the overture. My ears were still ringing from the rifles when a second and third volley went off. On the last volley, what appeared to be a ball fell from the roof above the audience. This was, in fact, a large colony of bats, which started to fly all around the huge church, swooping low over the crowd. Dave and I were in hysterics as we watched the terrified audience, many with their festival programmes over their heads to protect them. The band played on. Eventually the tiny pipistrelle bats began to leave the church through a small hole above the south porch. It was the talking point for a long time after the concert. I never did find out how Dave knew what was going to happen. At another concert soon afterwards, Dave and I counted eighty-nine bats out of the south porch hole. I also received a report that a sparrow hawk was hunting bats on a regular basis by perching in the trees near the south porch and swooping down fast on to the bats as they came out. I had never heard of this type of hunting by these very agile and fast aerial hunters, but on contacting the RSPB I discovered that this is quite common behaviour. At the time of writing this paragraph I still had not witnessed this spectacle, despite many evening observations.

My wildlife interests became well known both outside and within the force, and later in my service, a police role was to be created that was to change my life. This is the subject of the next chapter.

Police Wildlife Liaison Officer

In 1989 the Assistant Chief Constable of Essex at the time was Terry Rands – also a keen naturalist and very knowledgeable on wildlife law. He attended a concert at Thaxted Church and spoke to me at some length regarding the introduction of a police wildlife role within the force. He asked if I would be interested (and you can guess my reply). A few weeks later I was invited to police headquarters at Chelmsford to discuss the matter further with him. With the introduction of the Wildlife and Countryside Act in 1981 and legislation in the pipeline to protect badgers, more and more wildlife issues were being passed to the police. His idea was to appoint an officer within each division in the Essex Police District, who had some interest and/or knowledge of wildlife, whether it was birds, snakes, poaching offences or any other wildlife or countryside matter. These officers would be known as wildlife liaison officers and, as the title suggests, their main role was to liaise with wildlife organisations. The main groups were the Royal Society for the Protection of Birds (RSPB), the Royal Society for the Prevention of Cruelty to Animals (RSPCA), English Nature, the Ministry of Agriculture (MAFF), the Royal Society for Nature Conservation (RSNC) and local trust groups such as the Essex Wildlife Trust. My links were already well established with this trust and with the RSPB, but the list of organisations with which we were to maintain contact goes on and on.

I had a number of telephone conversations with Terry Rands on this subject before the scheme was launched at police headquarters in Essex in September 1991, with television and media present. I believe there were twenty-three officers present, including three senior officers, Terry Rands, Chief Superintendent Mick Brewer and Inspector Mick Barry. The media took a lot of interest in this new role within the police force, and soon after the launch I was contacted by local newspapers that featured front-page articles. I was also appointed as the police representative on the local Badger Protection Group which had been formed a few years prior to the WLO. In addition I became known as the Force Collator for Wildlife Offences such as egg stealing and badger baiting. Since that very early experience on the farm as a child, badgers have remained one of my favourite British mammals and, as the WLO role developed, badgers featured more and more.

Representing the force, I was fortunate enough to attend the first National Conference for Police Wildlife Liaison Officers, which was hosted by the RSPB. The WLO scheme was now national, with every force in the country having appointed WLOs. Some had appointed full-time officers, but a majority had followed our example in Essex and appointed a number of officers who would carry out their WLO duties in addition to their own specific duties. The annual conference became a very useful meeting place for WLOs from this country and abroad, particularly the Scandinavian countries. There were guest speakers from all walks of life within the wildlife scenario, from the Forensic Science Laboratory in Oregon, USA, specialising in wildlife offences and using the then relatively new concept of DNA analysis, to officers from the Wildlife Fisheries Department in the USA. The RSPB convened the first few annual conferences at various venues, normally Police Training Centres and on one occasion Bramshill Police Staff College, where senior police officers attend courses. More recently the annual conference has been taken over by the Department of the Environment.

Soon after the launch of the WLO in Essex, Terry Rands was approached by the Metropolitan Police WLO team, who were trying to set up a quarterly regional WLO conference to discuss cross-border intelligence on known criminals in wildlife matters. I was asked to attend this conference with two other Essex officers as the Essex representatives. This conference, which covers ten or more southern forces, has developed into an important link between them, and I have attended a majority of these. One of the conferences was attended by the Deputy Assistant Commissioner of the Metropolitan Police of the time, Michael Bradley-Taylor, who represented WLO interests for the Association of Chief Police Officers (ACPO) – an organisation directly answerable to the Home Office. He had recently attended an international conference on Wildlife Crime in Florida and reported to us that international wildlife crime was now the biggest money-making criminal activity, second only to drugs. A very sobering thought indeed.

The very first case that I dealt with as a WLO was a joint operation with the RSPCA and featured captive barn owls for sale. The case came to light as a result of an advertisement in a local paper, which was answered by a gentleman from Cambridge. He visited the house near Saffron Walden and became very concerned at the state of the birds. There were four owlets and two adult birds altogether. The adults were in a cage so small that they could not open their wings. The owlets were filthy dirty and looked subdued. He bought two owlets and took them straight to a vet in Cambridge, where it transpired that they were emaciated and had rickets. The gentleman reported the matter to the WLO in Cambridge, who contacted me with the details and a statement from the gentleman. Armed with the statement, I visited a local magistrate and swore out a warrant to visit the premises, where I seized the remaining birds. I took a series of photographs, which I later produced in court. The owner of the birds was prosecuted for a number of offences of cruelty and offences under the Wildlife and Countryside Act. He was fined and banned from keeping animals or birds for ten years. The media had a field day. The surviving birds were rehoused at an owl sanctuary in Shropshire. I was complimented by the chairman of the bench for the quality of the photographs – this being only the second case where I had used my own.

Almost at the same time that the WLO was launched, I was involved with two other rural officers in setting up a major police operation to deal with the growing number of illegal hare-coursing incidents. They were occurring on the rolling chalk hills on the Essex, Cambridge and Hertfordshire borders – effectively the entire northern border of our section. The incidents involved large groups of men who would descend on the area early in the morning. They would normally arrive on a Sunday between September and March, when the crops were low and the hares clearly visible. The men would line out with their greyhounds or lurcher-type dogs on slip leads and walk across the field, usually with two walking a short distance in front to make the next hare bolt. Huge amounts of money would be bet on the outcome of the course, either on the closest the dog came to the hare, or the hound that achieves the highest number of turns on the hare. The hare itself was rarely killed, as this was not their intention.

The problems arose mainly due to the damage caused to standing crops. When challenged by gamekeepers or landowners, the coursers would often become violent and some serious assaults were being reported as well as damage to vehicles – the coursers did not appreciate their 'sport' for the day being disrupted. This eventually resulted in a consortium of landowners writing to the Chief Constable of

Essex, asking for police assistance in dealing with the rapidly increasing problem. A senior lecturer at Anglia University was attached to me on the operation for almost two years. She was studying for a Masters Degree, and her thesis was a study on wildlife crime. She became a regular member of the team and was able to see the problems first-hand, sometimes too close for comfort.

After meetings with the consortium and police officers from the three forces involved, it soon became apparent in formulating a plan that it was going to be a cross-border operation. In those early days we had no four-wheel drive vehicles, so we were dependent on the cooperation of the landowners and gamekeepers who were all eager to assist. The plan was that one uniformed police officer would patrol in the keeper's vehicle, with the keeper driving. These vehicles were equipped with CB radios and backed up with police radios that each officer had. The CB (or Citizen Band) radio was all run on one channel and was coordinated by a farmer's wife in Cambridgeshire, who went by the call sign or 'handle' of 'Mother Hen'. Each vehicle also had a handle, mine being 'Fuzzy Bear', with reference to the beard. The entire operation like all police procedures had to have a name and this one was codenamed 'Operation Tortoise', with obvious reference to the famous fable.

From the very beginning we were kept busy. Keepers patrolling their own patch would find coursers, watch them to gather visual evidence of coursing and then call it in to Mother Hen. She would muster everyone and phone the police at the same time. We would all descend at the point and deal with the coursers. Once we had established who they were, which in the early days used to take ages, they were interviewed and recorded in a little notebook then reported for trespassing in pursuit of game. Often these checks would reveal that they were wanted somewhere else in the country, so we would arrest them and take them to

Saffron Walden Police Station, where the appropriate force would eventually collect them.

This did not please the custody sergeant at all, as the coursers would often arrive covered in mud and with boots absolutely laden in sticky clay. Operation Tortoise was the dread of the Sunday 'early turn' custody sergeant. A regular saying if the coursers were stopped on the motorway en route to our area was, 'It's all right, guv'nor, we aren't coursing in Essex. We don't want breakfast with the Essex Police.' I don't think anyone on the police side had really envisaged the scale of the problem, for a few weeks into the operation we were all preparing court papers against numerous coursers and every week more would arrive. I, for one, began to wonder if we would ever get on top of the problem.

One winter's morning we had been briefed at the base, which was one of the farms. There was a thick fog and we could see little across the fields. As dawn rose the first call of the day went up. Coursers had been sighted at Coplow Hills, a beautiful area of open rolling hills on the Essex/Cambridgeshire border – a favourite of the coursers. As we arrived we saw four vehicles parked on a grass verge. The tracks in the dew laden three-inch high wheat crop suggested that we had a big gang here. We were out in the middle of nowhere without any immediate police assistance in the area, so a call went out for back-up. Checks on the vehicles revealed that all four were from South London. As the keepers began to arrive, an apparition came out of the fog in the field and a sight that I will never forget.

There were nineteen men in a long line appearing initially in silhouette, walking towards us with dogs. It was reminiscent of a cowboy western, *The Showdown at Coplow Hills.* Some of them were huge and very menacing; it seemed even more so with only two of us there in uniform. Once again the adrenalin started to rush. Fortunately, as they reached us the cavalry arrived. Interviews began, but as three were wanted by other forces, two of which were for serious offences, and as others had given us false names and addresses, the decision was made to take them all in to Saffron Walden Police Station to verify their identities. The custody sergeant's nightmare began. On searching one of the men, he was found to be in possession of six thousand pounds in cash. He was the 'bet man' who would hold the cash for each course. Cambridgeshire Police beat that sum a few months later with a gentleman, who was detained at a coursing event in Linton, holding ten thousand pounds.

The incident with the nineteen coursers was not violent in any way, although they were angry at being caught and detained all day, as it took ages to process them all. Unfortunately, another incident that occurred a few months later was not so peaceful.

Early morning coursers had been spotted on fields between the M11 motorway and Coplow Hills. However, this gang had driven down a track and had partially concealed their vehicles in a hollow between fields. We all drove down the track to 'greet' them. There were four Subaru 4x4 estates parked up. The men ran back to their vehicles but we had them surrounded, except for one who decided to make a run for it. I was in a 4x4 pick-up used by the head keeper at the Audley End Estate. The keeper was driving and decided to pursue the fleeing vehicle, which was twisting and turning in the field which was dry for the time of year.

We kept trying to cut them off but without success. Suddenly, a rear window was opened. A catapult was held out and almost immediately a stone struck our windscreen and a split appeared. I called up for assistance but the other officers were dealing with the coursers left behind. Seven more stones were fired with deadly accuracy at our screen, which had now split in several places. We continued the pursuit and it became apparent that the Subaru was heading for a low hedge with a lane behind it. We could see a convoy of keepers' vehicles travelling along the road towards us and it looked as though the Subaru was on a collision course with the Land Rover that was the lead vehicle. Suddenly the Subaru crashed through the hedge, narrowly missing the Land Rover that had come to an abrupt halt. The Subaru turned violently left with a loud squeal of tyres. We followed and once again the adrenalin was rushing. The Subaru went along the lane with our car and the rest of the convoy in pursuit. A police Vauxhall Astra appeared behind us showing 'blues and twos' and we let it pass. It drew alongside the Subaru as we crossed over the motorway bridge. The Subaru turned abruptly into the side of the Astra but the Subaru came off worst as the front wing and driver's door completely caved in.

We stopped behind the two crashed cars and the convoy behind us passed on either side and surrounded them. Fortunately no one was injured. Had either of the cars crashed into the bridge railings and gone over, it could have been a lot more serious. We all got out and went to the Subaru. Initially the four men inside would not come out, but realising that their situation was hopeless, they emerged swearing and shouting at us. The front passenger was a huge man about six foot eight inches tall and built like a barn door. Subsequent enquiries on him revealed that he was well known to one of the south coast forces as a major drug dealer.

All of the men were convicted of a range of offences at the local magistrates court: these included damage to the crop in the field, damage to a police vehicle and the windscreen of the pick-up that I had been in, hare coursing, and reckless driving. The latter was for the driver of the Subaru and he was disqualified from driving for two years. All four received heavy fines and huge compensation awards were made against each of them.

News of this and other cases spread through the coursing

fraternity with features on several television networks including BBC, Carlton, ITV and a French network. I was even interviewed for a big article in the hallowed pages of *The Times* newspaper. The coursers started to get the message, at least in Hertfordshire, Essex and Cambridge, that their activities would not be tolerated. They moved their pitches and began to course further north in Suffolk, Lincolnshire and Bedfordshire.

Several years on, the operation is still running but has been scaled down to one police vehicle patrolling the area. Of course the keepers and landowners are ever vigilant and we must not forget 'Mother Hen'.

Over the years since the inception of wildlife liaison officers, I have had numerous incidents passed on to me and I am now going to relate just a few, some of which are amusing and some tragic.

A lesser spotted woodpecker was brought into Great Dunmow Police Station one afternoon, having been rescued from a cat. It appeared uninjured but could not fly. A vet examination revealed that the cat had punctured the bird's pectoral muscles (these are the muscles that extend across a bird's chest) and the puncture meant that, when the bird's wing was extended and the muscle expanded, the bird became uncomfortable. I took it home in a box and Pat, my second wife, and I scratched our heads as we were unsure what to feed it on. Suddenly, I remembered that the local garage had a maggot machine for the fishermen, and for the next ten days the woodpecker ate a pot and a half each day. The garage owner approached Pat one day and enquired as to what we were doing with all the maggots. Her reply was, 'Barry's changed his diet'! After ten days the bird had fully recovered and I released it in a local wood close to our house, as I did not want to risk it meeting the cat again.

On another occasion a local farmer who had managed to

release an adult tawny owl that had been trapped down his chimney for a week contacted me in the evening. He had placed the bird on his lawn but it was so weak that it simply fell over. It was mid-winter and cold. We brought the bird home and kept it in the downstairs toilet in a box, as we had no indoor aviary. We force-fed it for two days on raw breast of chicken (only the best!) and with the food and warmth it soon perked up. Some of our neighbours brought round shrews and mice that the cats had left, and the owl needed little encouragement to eat them. After seven days the bird was fully restored to health and was taken back to the farm where it was found and released. (It is particularly important that owls are released back into their own territories.)

The very day we decided to release the tawny owl, I was contacted by a local gentleman who informed me that he had a snowy owl in his garden and it appeared to be very weak. My initial reaction was that it was a barn owl, but on attending the garden I found that the man was right and an adult snowy was under his tree. With some difficulty I managed to catch the bird, but as I placed it in a box in the car, I had forgotten how sharp their inch long talons were. One sank deep into my hand and another went through the edge of my wrist and out the other side. (Boy, did that hurt!) The bird was a magnificent female. A keeper from a local wildlife park collected her and placed her with a number of other snowy owls before her owner later collected her. My injuries took a while to heal and I subsequently invested in a pair of leather gauntlets.

I seem to have had a lot to do with owls. I was once contacted by the animal warden for the District Council, who was about to visit a gentleman regarding a complaint of 'noisy owls' and he asked if I would go along as he knew nothing about the licensing and keeping of owls. We found three large aviaries in a line in the gentleman's garden. The central aviary, which was the largest, contained a magnificent pair of snowy owls. The two adjoining aviaries contained barn owls. The problem was that it was early spring and the barn owls were very territorial. The two pairs were swearing at each other all through the night and one of the neighbours had recorded the cacophony – you think cats can make a noise! The poor old snowies were quiet and innocent. The gentleman fully accepted the problem and resolved it by selling one of the pairs, which he replaced with a Bengalese eagle owl. He was a real owl enthusiast.

Once a local farmer friend of mine who had discovered some dead trout in his reservoir contacted me. He initially suspected that they might have been killed deliberately, as he had recently increased the rod licences for the syndicate that fished there. It was a sad sight that greeted me when I attended. He had scooped out some of the dead fish, some of which were a lovely size, while others were gasping for air on the surface. It was February time and not particularly warm, but despite this the first impressions were that the fish were suffocating, as their gills were protruding out from under the gill flaps. The Ministry of Agriculture and the Environment Agency were called in to take water samples and to carry out tests on some of the dead fish. If they had been poisoned deliberately it must have been a pretty powerful chemical, for within two days over one thousand fish were dead. The tests revealed high levels of phosphate algae and the Ministry established that local farmers had been spreading a phosphate fertiliser on the fields, which had subsequently frozen on the surface. Rain had then washed this fertiliser into the local river, from which the owner of the reservoir had pumped water out to top up his reservoir. This phosphate-rich water had then produced the algae that reduced the oxygen levels in the reservoir to a critical level for the fish and they suffocated – an interesting but sad case.

One spring I wrote an article in the local press regarding snakes, as I had received a number of telephone calls from concerned members of the public. I pointed out that the vast majority of snakes found in north-west Essex are harmless grass snakes that will normally live near water. Adders are rarely found in this area, as they prefer sandy heaths. The article had the opposite effect to that which I had intended and calls came flooding in. The grass snakes had obviously had a very prosperous breeding season the previous year and had successfully hibernated through the mild winter. They were turning up everywhere.

A report of an eight-foot long 'anaconda' in a pond at Thaxted turned out to be a beautiful four-foot long grass snake, which I removed to the pond of a friend of mine, who was a snake enthusiast. A 'boa constrictor' arrived in a lady's garage and as a local collector had reported one missing, I took the dog catcher to investigate. This is simply a length of pipe with a rope running through it and a loop at one end that can be tightened. I opened the up-and-over garage door carefully but could not see the huge snake I was looking for. However, under a box in the corner was a twelve-inch long baby grass snake. The elderly lady was absolutely terrified of snakes. I think this is a trait of human nature that when frightened of something the size and description is exaggerated.

One afternoon my colleague and I were drinking a cup of tea at the police station, a rare habit of policemen, when the phone rang. A member of the public was reporting a stag deer trapped in a cricket net on a local sports ground. Thinking that it was simply trapped inside a practice run, we went out to investigate. The sight that greeted us was quite unbelievable. A large, fully antlered fallow buck had managed to become entwined in the netting of the practice net. It had struggled for a while, twisting and turning, so that the net had formed a huge ball around the antlers. This had eventually tightened to such an extent that the terrified animal was on its knees and panting heavily. As we approached, it managed to stand up and began thrashing around in fear. With hind legs kicking and head being thrown violently from side to side, there was obviously danger at both ends of the animal. We had by this time been joined by two men who happened to be passing and decided that the only way to free the buck was to try and cut the net off the antlers that were barely visible. That is when the fun began.

With some difficulty I managed to grab the net ball with both hands and tried to twist the deer's head with the intention of getting it on to the ground. The deer did not understand of course and fought furiously against me. It took all my strength and more to fight it but eventually I won and it went down still thrashing violently. The two men then assisted by sitting carefully on the deer to prevent it getting up again. With a pocket knife, my colleague began to cut though the net that was three or four inches thick between the antlers. I held on for dear life (pardon the pun) as the frightened animal continued to try and thrash around. It was a good fifteen minutes before the last of the netting ball fell free and there was a thick carpet on the ground.

Then came the difficult bit – releasing the magnificent animal without injury to ourselves. With a superbly synchronised movement, I let go as the two men got up. I leapt to my feet almost as quickly as the deer. It ran off across the park and stopped about five hundred yards from us between two mature oak trees that shone in the autumn sun. The buck looked back at us for a full minute before running off and disappearing over the horizon. (I would like to think that it had stopped to say thanks!) It was a lovely moment to see this most magnificent of beasts running freely once more. My arms and shoulders ached for several days afterwards and I discovered muscles that I never knew I had, but it was worth the effort.

One morning I found a box that had been left outside the door of the Thaxted Police Office. I opened it gingerly only to find a huge grass snake coiled up inside. There was nothing to indicate the name or address of the finder or any details of where it had been found. At four and a half feet long, it was one of the biggest specimens I had seen. I rang a local farmer who had a large pond on his farm and he agreed that I could release it there. It glided across the water and disappeared amongst the bulrushes on the other side. It was seen again several weeks later basking on the bank of the pond.

For the benefit of the next stories, it would help the reader to understand the term 'imprinting'. In birds, this is simply when another bird of different breed, or a human being, fosters a very young bird. In both cases, the young bird grows up accepting its surrogate parent as its parent, mate and pal.

North American ferruginous hawks are large and quite magnificent birds of prey, which are popular with raptor keepers in Britain. At the time that this incident occurred, it was required that the birds be licensed with the Department of the Environment at Bristol.

I received a report from a concerned member of the public that one of these hawks was being kept in a van in the area. Along with the local RSPCA inspector, I visited the premises early one morning. The van was parked outside but there was no bird inside it. We called at the house and were invited in. There was the magnificent hawk sitting on a perch. The bird's name was Gorbash after the dragon in the story 'Flight of Dragons'. There was no licence for the bird and initially the owner would not tell us where he had bought it. Therefore, I had no option but to report him for the offence and seize the bird, which was collected and cared for by an organisation known as 'Raptor Rescue'. Within a few days I received an urgent call to say that the bird was not eating and was showing signs of stress. It was Raptor Rescue that identified the problem – it transpired that the bird had imprinted on the owner. As the bird's welfare was paramount, the owner received a caution by the local police inspector, who incidentally, had never cautioned someone for this offence before. A licence was issued and the bird was reunited with the owner who told us that he had bought Gorbash for three hundred and fifty pounds in a pub in London. The bird soon recovered from its ordeal.

The second incident involved a female kestrel, a small British falcon that hunts for food by hovering over hedges and grassland and is regularly seen over the grass embankments of motorways. I had received an anonymous letter alleging that a fourteen-year-old boy had a kestrel in an aviary at a local address. I called at the house and spoke to the boy who showed me the bird, which was fit and healthy and hand tame. Initially, the boy would not tell me where the bird had come from but he later admitted that he had taken it from a nest as a very young bird and had reared it. This is a specific offence under the Wildlife and Countryside Act, another being that the bird had not been registered. The boy was reported for these offences and the bird was seized. It soon became apparent that the bird was under stress and that it had imprinted on the boy, who received a caution and a licence from the Department of the Environment. You may feel that the boy had got away with it and that the police were condoning the taking of wild birds from the wild, but we were left with no real alternative as the bird's welfare and future were the main concern. Every case must be taken on its individual merits.

Having received a number of complaints of herons visiting garden ponds during the winter months, when food can be scarce for them and with requests for advice on how to deter them, I wrote an article in the local press. I pointed out, amongst other things, that they are protected and one deterrent was a line suspended about nine inches high around the outside of the pond. It had worked on our two ponds where herons had previously been regular visitors.

About two weeks after this report was published I received a telephone call at home one evening from the mother of two boys. The account was that the boys had been out in a field behind some bungalows when they had found a dead heron. As they picked it up a lady from a nearby garden said, 'It's all right boys, my husband shot it.' I met the boys the following day and they took me to the field, having previously spoken to the landowner. As I entered the field with the boys, I saw a man enter it from a garden of one of the bungalows. He was pulling up his trousers and trying to tuck his shirt in – he obviously had not seen us. I told the boys to stay where they were and approached the man who was rushing across the field through the long grass. He reached down and picked up the dead heron, its wings drooped lifelessly blowing in the wind. He turned back towards the bungalow and caught sight of me. He mouthed some unrepeatable expletive and tried to hide the bird behind his back. The bird's wings were hanging out either side of his trousers, which were slowly falling down and his shirt tails were blowing in the wind. I seized the bird and advised him to get dressed before I cautioned him. In the subsequent interview he admitted shooting the bird that had been visiting his large ornamental pond and had taken some of his young koi carp. He also admitted knowing that they were protected. He appeared at the local magistrates court where he was fined one hundred and fifty pounds with fifty pounds costs, and subsequently police headquarters revoked his shotgun certificate.

A local farmer friend once brought an unusual find round to the house, a beautiful swift that had flown into a window-pane and appeared to be concussed. It would have been very difficult if not impossible to force-feed it, so we placed it in a bucket half full of straw, covered it over and left it for the night, fully expecting to find it dead the following day. It looked quite pitiful in the bucket with its impressive sickle-shaped wings outstretched on the straw and its spindle legs hardly able to support it. The following morning a wonder-ful sight greeted us: the bird was bright and perky. Pat gently lifted it out of the bucket and placed it on her hand. We then noticed a large spider-like creature under the feathers behind the neck. We assumed that it was a creature that the bird had picked up from the straw, and with some difficulty I removed it. We stood in the garden and Pat simply lifted her outstretched hand to the sky and the bird took flight, need-ing little encouragement. It was a beautiful early morning with a blue sky and another magical moment was recorded. What made it more remarkable was the fact that if it was a male bird it would probably never land again. The insect that I had removed from the swift's feathers I later learned was a parasitic wingless fly that lives on birds. The insect was quite grotesque when viewed under a hand lens.

People often ask me why it is that cats will bring home shrews and play with them until the hapless creatures die, but the antagonist will not eat them. I am told that they are bitter to the taste, although I have never tried one! This leads me nicely on to an amusing incident involving a mole, which are also apparently bitter to the taste.

I was at home and off duty one morning when I answered the telephone. A terrified lady was on the other end and I feared the worst, a serious assault or something equally ter-rible. It took me a while to calm her down enough to estab-lish what the problem was. I had already grabbed the police car keys, as I assumed that whatever it was I was going to be racing out. I eventually established between tears and the panic breathing that her cat had brought in a live mole and placed it on the linoleum floor of the lady's kitchen, whilst she was washing up at the sink. On seeing the mole she had given out an almighty scream and run out of the kitchen. At the same time the mole had scuttled away under the cooker and the cat had beaten a hasty retreat out the back door. I attended thinking that it would be a simple job of removing the 'monster'. As you have probably gathered by now, the lady was absolutely terrified of rodents of any description. With some difficulty I managed to pull the cooker out and there it was, but before I could reach forward to grab it, it had scuttled through a gap behind the fitted cupboard on its huge spade-like front feet. On opening the cupboard door I realised that the mole was in fact in the cupboard, so I then had to remove all the pots, pans, bowls and utensils. As the last bits came out the mole exited as it had entered and scuttled across the floor, only to disappear behind the fridge freezer. This weighed a ton as I managed to ease it out but at the same time the mole decided to come out of its own accord and hide behind the washing machine. I pulled that out being careful not to disconnect any of the pipes but the mole had once again disappeared through a narrow gap into another cupboard. Yes, you've guessed it, a fully stocked food cupboard! I was beginning to lose my patience. Out came all the food but this time I had blocked the hole where it had entered. The floor of the kitchen was rapidly turning into a war zone. In the meantime the mole had left that cupboard and gone into the one next door through another gap. (They were not well fitted cupboards!) I blocked the gap up and started to empty the next cupboards that were full of heavy Le Creuset pans.

At last I had him cornered, or so I thought. I reached in to grab him but he scuttled under my arm, out of the cupboard and on to the floor. He scampered through all the debris and disappeared down the side of the tumble dryer. I really was beginning to dislike this mole. I pulled the dryer out and there he was, trapped. He had nowhere to go but past me. I had grabbed a towel, and as he made a dash for it, I dropped the towel over him, fell to my knees and quickly cupped my gloved hands over him. I carefully carried the mole to the sink, thinking that if it did escape, it would be trapped in the sink. With some difficulty I managed to remove it from the towel and it immediately bit straight through my regulation police issue gloves and deep into my finger. I examined the mole to see if the cat had injured it but it appeared unharmed. There was no blood on its dense black fur, which was once prized for collars on coats and other garments. I carried it out into the garden and through to a field beyond, where the cat was nowhere to be seen. There were a lot of molehills in the grass and when I placed the wriggling mole down, off he scuttled. He had not moved far when he began to dig, and the speed with which he disappeared was quite remarkable. I returned to the bombsite, which was previously the kitchen floor and called out to the lady to let her know the mole was gone. Her face when she came into the kitchen was a real picture. I helped her tidy everything away and she was very grateful, as she readily admitted she suffered with a phobia of rodents. My finger had stopped bleeding but it was painful for several days – a salutary lesson to wear stronger gloves. I now use industrial leather gauntlets for birds of prey and mammals.

Whilst on nights we were sent to an alarm at a local village church at 3 a.m. It was an 'immediate response' call, so two police cars arrived with blue lights flashing. A check of the outside of the church revealed no obvious break-in. The vicar and church warden duly arrived and we all went in. A thorough search showed nothing amiss. The reason for the alarm activation was therefore a mystery. I suggested to the vicar that bats might have set it off – a suggestion that was dismissed by both vicar and church warden. I advised them that there are very few old churches in Essex or in fact in the country that do not have bats in residence, either all the time or at certain times of the year. The vicar dismissed this until I showed him the tiny little droppings similar in appearance to those of the mouse, but when handled they are dry and crumbly. I carefully crushed a few in the palm of my hand and showed him the tiny wing cases and other indigestible insect parts that had passed through the bats. He was quite fascinated, and since that night the vicar contacted the local bat group, who have identified the species of bats for him as the pipistrelle. The cause of the alarm activation was blamed on the bats.

Whilst walking the dogs one day off duty, I received a call from a very concerned office clerk at Braintree Police Station. A gentleman had walked in to the front office and deposited a small box on the counter. The clerk had the fright of her life when she opened it as it contained a black scorpion. The gentleman had purchased a box of nectarines at a local car boot sale the day before, taken them home, and on emptying them out into his fruit bowl had discovered the creature in the bottom. I suggested one of the local zoos but once again the RSPCA came to the rescue. A warning notice was published in the local press.

A pair of pied wagtails caused a few problems to Essex Police at Stansted Airport when they built a nest in the mobile communications trailer, which is permanently sited at the Emergency Rendezvous Point at the airport. The radio engineers at headquarters wanted to move the trailer to service it. The female wagtail was sitting on eggs and was not going to move. One of my colleagues rang me to ascertain what the law was in respect of disturbance of the nest and I informed him that the trailer could not be moved and no work could commence on it until the adults had fledged their young. This was reiterated to a chief inspector who rang me from headquarters. Therefore the service was delayed by six weeks and there were no 'full emergencies' at the airport during that time!

Search warrants can sometimes turn up the most unusual items. One of my Cm colleagues rang me one afternoon for advice. She had been executing a search warrant at a local house primarily for firearms and drugs but had turned up an egg collection in excess of one hundred eggs. They were seized and handed over to me to deal with. There was no data or identification with the collection, so I took them over to the RSPB headquarters at Sandy, Bedfordshire, where they were all identified. Two eggs were listed in Schedule 1 of the Wildlife and Countryside Act 1999 and therefore afforded special protection. (Of course, egg collecting is now illegal under this act.) The person concerned, incidentally, was subsequently sentenced to twelve years' imprisonment for several serious offences including paedophile activities. A confiscation order was made on the egg collection and, with the data provided by the RSPB, the collection was handed over to the local wildlife trust for educational purposes.

Domestic disputes between married couples are the bane of any policeman's life, as we are not allowed to become involved unless offences have occurred such as assault or breach of the peace. In this particular situation, the husband had left his wife, moved to London and started divorce proceedings. He had left a horse with his estranged wife at their fourteen-acre smallholding, and when he had visited the premises the horse was gone. He reported the alleged theft of the horse along with the fact that there were a large number of dogs in the house. I attended but there was no one at the premises and no horse. The house was, however, full of dogs and there was excrement all over the inside of the windows. On lifting up the postal flap the smell that wafted out was unbelievable. I left the house and contacted the husband who was in the process of having his estranged wife evicted on a court order. He had purchased her a flat in London and the question of the horse was left as a civil matter between them. The reason I have mentioned this was that four weeks later I was called back to the house by the husband who wanted to show me the inside of it.

He met me outside and suggested that I put wellingtons on. The sight that greeted me inside was beyond belief and quite nauseating. The ground floor was two inches deep in a slurry form of dog excrement throughout. The settee and armchairs were hardly recognisable as such. The walls were plastered. It was tricky to walk, as the steps could not be seen. The stairs were deep in the slurry that was very slowly creeping down. The gentleman invited me upstairs but I declined. I had seen enough, especially when I looked up at the ceilings in the kitchen and lounge. There were huge dark brown stains in the artex. There is an old saying in the police service that after visiting some houses you have to wipe your feet on the way out – I never thought I would see that come true. I had to wash my boots off thoroughly after leaving, and when I returned to the police car, my colleague who had declined to come into the house refused to get in the car with me. I had to air my clothes as the smell was so overpowering – she should have come into the house! It appeared that the woman lived in the house with forty-odd dogs, which she never allowed out to answer the call of nature. She had left the country and was living in San Francisco with her new partner. We gave up looking for her.

One Christmas Eve, I was off duty at the police house, when

a gentleman called at the office door. He reported that he had just driven back from Elsenham Railway Station to Thaxted and approximately three miles from the railway station an ostrich had run across his path. It was dark and he had clearly seen it in his headlights. My immediate reaction was, 'Oh yes, sir. And what have we had to drink tonight, then?' He had thought that I may respond this way but he had not drunk a thing. My control room thought that I had been drinking when I phoned it in. 'And a happy Christmas to you as well, officer,' was the reaction from the duty inspector. It subsequently transpired that the bird had actually escaped from an ostrich farm some miles away and was recaptured three days later.

Whilst on the subject of unusual sightings, I must mention the issue of the big cat sightings that have occurred from time to time all over the country, including Essex and the north-west of the county. At this point I have to confess that I remain very sceptical. I will not believe it until I actually see one myself or one is found dead on the road. In over twenty-five years that sightings have been reported, not one animal has been killed on the roads. I find it difficult to believe that a cat the size of a leopard or puma can remain concealed in the fairly densely populated south-east of England and not be spotted on a more regular basis, as it patrols its five hundred square mile territory. Some of the sightings that we have had from farmers and gamekeepers have been quite impressive but I'm afraid that I am still not personally convinced.

I have been the convenor of the annual conference for Essex Wildlife Liaison Officers for a number of years, arranging speakers and venues. One guest speaker was a national wildcat expert who was studying the distribution and numbers of wild cats in Britain. He had assisted several forces that had problems with loose large wild cats, which invariably turned out to be escapees from private collections.

He gave a very interesting presentation to the conference with video and photographic evidence of dead animals killed by large cats, together with impressive statistical data on sightings throughout the country over a number of years. With no disrespect to anyone who may have seen one, or to the experts who say that we do have a problem in this country with large wild cats, I remain to date a doubting Thomas, but expect one day to have to eat these words.

By way of conclusion to this chapter, I will relate three recent cases, which may be of interest to the reader. The first concerns great crested newts, which are now protected by national and European law. This level of protection has come about as a result of a drastic decline in numbers since the Second World War, not only in Britain but also throughout Europe. Many breeding ponds have been filled in and much land drained, both for agriculture and development. These factors along with pollution mean that the newts have reduced in numbers, hence the level of protection given to these lovely creatures. Not only are the newts themselves protected but their habitats as well.

Great crested newts are amphibians and like others such as the frog and toad, need water to breed and to develop their tadpoles. The adults arrive in the ponds as early as January and as late as June. Here they will mate and the female will lay several hundred eggs on the underside of aquatic leaves. Like frogs and toads, they will normally return to the same pond to breed each year. Usually by mid-July, the adults will have left the ponds and will be actively feeding in preparation for hibernating in late autumn. By this time, the tadpoles will have developed lungs and legs and would be leaving the ponds to hibernate under logs, stones and anything to protect them from the rigours of the winter. (Remember our findings in the cellar of the farm in Chapter One?) They may have to travel up to five hundred yards from the breeding pond or stream to feed and hibernate, and the cycle restarts the following spring.

It is against this background of the biology of the great crested newt and their level of protection that this case came about. It was early one autumn that the secretary of a local Natural History Society contacted me. They expressed concern at the proposed development of a large grass meadow site that had an old derelict building in the centre that bats frequented. However, their main worry was that great crested newts also used the site, which was strewn with fallen trees and general debris, offering excellent hibernation sites. The newts bred in several ponds, both natural and purpose-built garden ponds around the periphery of the site. I was asked to examine some of the garden ponds, and sure enough there were young great crested newts in varying stages of losing their gills as their lungs developed. I contacted English Nature, as there was obvious presence of newts and the bats in the building – both were protected species. They had already received an application from an ecologist employed by the developer to carry out a detailed survey of the whole site and present a report. English Nature decided to bring in their own herpetologist and mammal expert to carry out a similar survey. Both species were found and the developers were given advice. A four-acre part of the site, which had the densest population of newts and the most fallen willow trees, was to be left by the developers.

Whilst the newts were all hibernating, a 'newt-proof' fence was erected all around the site under development, to prevent them from returning to a large pond in the middle of the site, which was to be developed and was destined to be filled in. However, this fence did not prevent the newts from gaining access to the numerous garden ponds already in existence and a natural pond at the far end of the area, which had been left. The following spring the Natural History Society in the village carried out a survey under licence by English

Nature to establish how the population and distribution of newts had been affected by the development that was well under way safely behind the newt-proof fence. The survey revealed a record number of newts in all the ponds surveyed – it was obvious that they had not been adversely affected by being displaced by the barrier around the site.

Throughout the summer, work continued on the site as the fifty houses rose with incredible speed. Everything was running smoothly, even the bats had found another roost in a farm barn nearby where they had not been seen before. English Nature were making regular visits and were more than satisfied with the breeding success of the newts and the efforts made by the developers.

As autumn set in, the newts started to leave the ponds and return to the site that had been set aside for them. This had been further improved by the depositing of some of the rubble from the derelict buildings that had been demolished. There was no sign that the newts had scaled the newt-proof fence or managed to dig underneath it, as the specifications provided by English Nature stated that the plastic had to be buried to a depth of twelve inches. Everyone was pleased with the progress so far.

However, the tranquillity turned into a storm in early December of that year. It was a Saturday morning and I was on hunt duty at the other side of the county on the coast. It was a bright sunny morning with a gentle inshore breeze. We had no sabs, the hounds could not find the scent of a fox and all was at peace with the world – until my mobile rang. The secretary of the Natural History Society was very distressed. It would appear that the developers had driven over the newt-proof fence with two huge bulldozers and were clearing and levelling the newts' hibernation site. I called up on the police car radio and asked them to send a car to the site and ascertain exactly what was going on. I had to give a brief résumé of the situation before I rang the secretary back. She was in tears but did have the foresight to obtain a video camera and film the activities whilst someone else was taking stills. There was little more I could do apart from answering a dozen calls from some very angry naturalists. By the time the police car arrived at the site, having had to deal with a road traffic accident en route, the bulldozers had cleared the site and the drivers had gone home. It transpired that no one could actually get on the site to stop them because of an eight-foot high security fence. The damage was done but I just could not understand what the developers were up to. They had cooperated well all the way through – up until now it seemed.

I walked into a storm of protest when I arrived for work at 9 a.m. the following Monday morning. I started taking statements, while English Nature surveyed the damage. All of the trees had been piled up in one corner and the bulldozer blade had skimmed off the top grass layer, leaving exposed dirt on a completely level surface. I took statements from everyone who had witnessed the bulldozers working and seized the video film and exposed film for developing. The following day I contacted the site agent and advised him that I needed to see him. He arranged for the company solicitor to be present at the interview, which was booked for a few days hence. Interestingly enough, there were no dead newts found on the site but it was assumed that they had been scooped up when the bulldozers scraped off the surface. In view of that, I was forced to concentrate on the destruction of the habitat.

At the subsequent interview, the solicitor instructed the site agent to make no comment and the site agent was reported as a representative of the company for destruction of the habitat. Later, covert enquiries revealed that it had been ground clearance subcontractors who had decided to take it upon themselves to clear the newt site. They thought they were doing the firm a favour by clearing it as they considered it an eyesore with all the trees lying around mingled with debris. They were apparently not aware of the issue of the newts, albeit that they had driven over their fence. The site agent was so upset by what had happened that he left the site. He had taken a keen interest in the newts and their progress.

Having gathered a total of sixteen statements and all the evidence I considered to be relevant to the case, I submitted case papers to the Crown Prosecution Service (CPS). There had to date only been one other case brought under the European Habitat Regulations and the Wildlife and Countryside Act, and this had resulted in the conviction of the developer in the north-east who received a fine of seventy thousand pounds. The file was returned for a few amendments – very few files reach the CPS without bouncing at least once – and subsequently resubmitted. It was shortly after this that I sustained a serious injury to my right foot involving torn tendons and ligaments, when I was required to kick a door in at the house of an elderly gentleman who had not been seen for some days; sadly the man had died. I was off work for almost a year as tendon damage takes a long time to repair. On returning to work I contacted the CPS to ascertain the progress of the 'newt case.' It was then that it became apparent that the file had in fact gone missing. An enquiry was launched but it never resurfaced and the statute of limitation meant that the case was now out of time. I was very disturbed as a lot of work had gone into the case, and many other people were disappointed with this outcome.

The second case involved cruelty to horses on a massive scale. In January 1998, the Secretary of the American Quarter Horse Association received an anonymous letter. It alleged that there were a large number of horses being kept in cruel conditions at large stables in a remote area of north Essex. The matter was passed to the RSPCA, who in turn contacted me for assistance. The likelihood of obtaining a warrant to search the premises was quite remote on anonymous information but it was decided that we would visit the premises regardless. Arrangements were made with the RSPCA and members of the British Horse Society (BHS). A meeting was held at the local police station, prior to visiting the stables, and everyone was fully briefed. It was a cold dull January morning when the convoy of vehicles arrived at the stables. The female owner was there and invited us in. When I spoke to her and advised her of the nature of our visit, she made no objections.

In the very first stable we found a small black Shetland pony called Nobby. He was lying down in the dirty straw and a closer examination revealed that he was unable to stand up, as his hooves were so overgrown and deformed. I grabbed my camera and requested a vet. Unfortunately, the woman owed money to every vet in the local area, so one was requested from Bedfordshire. While we waited for him, we continued our examination. We found a large number with grossly overgrown hooves and on one animal it had gone right over on to the side of its fetlocks. A large grey mare called Kiri had a huge lump on the side of her face, which had dislodged her eye. The lump was weeping from a hole near the animal's nostrils. This lump proved to be a malignant tumour. An American Quarter Horse stallion called Jefferson appeared to be having difficulty breathing and I later learned that he was suffering from Chronic Obstructive Airways Disease (COPD). The general condition of most of the horses was not good, many having very overgrown hooves. The senior representative of the BHS, Mr Ivan Morgan, stated that, in over forty years of working with horses and the BHS, he had never seen anything like it.

The vet duly arrived and commenced his examination. On seeing Nobby he decided to shoot him to prevent any further suffering to the poor creature. He also expressed concern for Jefferson but decided to let him live and see if he would respond to treatment. He stated that the tumour on Kiri's face was in his view too far gone for her to be saved but a local horse rescue centre collected her and offered treatment. The result of his examination of the remaining twenty-nine horses revealed that in his view there were a further seven animals that were in such a condition causing 'unnecessary suffering' – an offence under The Protection of Animals Act, 1911, Section 1.

Whilst the BHS made arrangements for the seven animals to be taken away for urgent treatment, I formally interviewed the woman and reported her for the offences. The local rescue centre took Kiri away and the remainder were collected at 7 p.m. when a large horsebox arrived from the BHS's headquarters in Warwickshire. It was decided to leave Jefferson to see if he would respond to treatment, as it was believed that his condition might have been brought on partly by the poor quality of the hay that he was being fed.

I will never forget the sight of the little Shetlands, some of whom had never been let out of their stables. They struggled with excitement as they tottered on their overgrown feet across the yard to the lorry that was about to transport them to a better life. They had great difficulty in climbing the ramp into the lorry. One Shetland mare called Rosie had hooves that were so overgrown that she was walking on her fetlocks. She had difficulty even moving and I had a big lump in my throat. I felt as if I wanted to rush over, pick her up and carry her to the lorry – if I had been strong enough I probably would have done so. It was a very pathetic sight and one that I hope I will never see again. Shetlands are my favourite breed of pony as they are full of spirit. I always think of them as the Jack Russell terriers of the horse world, which made it even worse seeing them reduced to this state. It was a long and traumatic day for everyone concerned.

In case you are wondering about Jefferson and the other

horses that were left behind, the act at this time did not allow us power of seizure for the animals that appeared not to be suffering unnecessarily. However, the BHS and the RSPCA did offer assistance to the lady, which was accepted. A vet at the rescue centre she had been taken to examined Kiri. The tumour was so bad that it was decided to end the horse's suffering and she was put down. The animals that went to Warwickshire commenced a long-term treatment programme on their feet that would take up to three years before the animals were able to walk properly again. I was sent some photographs of them in the fields grazing and they looked really happy. Sadly, however, little Rosie was not so lucky. A vet's examination revealed that under her thick ginger coat she was painfully thin; his actual description was skeletal. She did not respond to treatment and a further examination confirmed their suspicions that she was suffering from the advanced stages of stomach and bowel cancer. Once again the decision was made to have her put down. Jefferson responded to treatment and I visited him a few weeks afterwards when he was fine, so much so in fact that he tried to bite my colleague's arm as he leaned on the stable door.

Case papers with over fifty photographs were submitted to the Crown Prosecution Service and a CPS solicitor who had extensive knowledge of horses took on the case. The case was finally heard some fourteen months later at Chelmsford Magistrates Court. It was a three-day trial, as the lady concerned was pleading not guilty. Evidence was heard from three vets, the BHS farrier and members of the BHS that had accompanied me on the initial visit. The BHS had been invaluable in the investigation, particularly Ivan Morgan. In defence, the lady brought three character and expert witnesses, but when they were shown the photographs, they had to agree that the animals had been neglected and were suffering unnecessarily – these last two words were crucial in this case. The eventual verdict was guilty on all eight charges of causing unnecessary suffering to animals in her charge. The court adjourned for four weeks to consider sentence. I was expecting some form of ban and a fine and I was therefore surprised that when she reappeared she was sent to prison for two months. She was also disqualified from keeping horses for ten years and ordered to pay costs of almost four thousand pounds – a successful conclusion to a very sad case that I shall never forget. The case had attracted a lot of media attention and I was interviewed by national television outside the court and by local radio and newspapers as well. Many of my photographs appeared on TV and in the papers during the following weeks. The images of the shetlands struggling across the yard to the lorry will remain with me always. I am not generally an emotional person in respect of animals, having worked in a zoo and on the farm, but that moment did bring tears to my eyes.

As this case was proceedings to its conclusion, I was involved in another horse cruelty case, this time involving a five-year-old shire horse stallion. The animal warden for Epping Forest District Council had been delivering some stray dogs to a kennel near Saffron Walden when she had noticed a very thin shire horse standing in a field. She rang the police control room at Chelmsford, who in turn contacted myself and the local RSPCA Inspector. We both arrived at the farm at the same time. The horse was in a field on its own, standing near a fence. The owner, a young lady, accompanied us across the field to the horse, which appeared painfully thin. The ribs, hindquarters and backbone were clearly visible. A horsebox was summoned for the horse to be taken for treatment. The poor creature was led to the box but was very unsteady on its feet. On reaching the ramp of the box it fell over and simply lay on its side, unable to even lift its head. The decision was then taken to put the animal out of its misery there and then.

At the time of ending this chapter I am embroiled in a major case of cruelty involving a number of puppies and adult dogs and puppy farms in Wales. I can say little more as the case is sub judice, but it may appear in a sequel.

I will conclude this chapter on a lighter note, involving me more in my role as a naturalist than a police wildlife liaison officer. The story, which I can assure you is true, although seemingly unbelievable, involves a pair of blackbirds. A friend of mine in Thaxted rang me one day stating that these blackbirds had built a nest in the engine of her car close to the battery. Not unusual in itself you might think, but when I took my camera down to photograph the nest and four fledglings, the full story unfolded.

The car had been used to take the lady's two young boys to Cambridge to school everyday – a round trip of forty-four miles twice a day. When the birds started to build the nest, the lady and her husband naturally thought that the disturbance of the two trips would deter the birds from continuing their nest construction, but it did not. The birds would just sit on the couple's fence until the car returned and they would then continue building. Four eggs were laid in the nest and – yes you've guessed it – when the lady got into the car to commence the journey to Cambridge, the female bird would simply hop out under the wheel arch on to the tyre and up on to the fence. On the car's return she would go back to her incubating duties. I can only assume that the heat of the engine kept the uncovered eggs warm. When the lady's husband's firm heard the story, they took sympathy on the blackbirds and hired a car for the lady to use for six weeks until the young were successfully fledged. The nest was then removed from the engine and was placed in the garden hedge but it was not reused. So that is another incredible story that I would not have believed if I had not seen it with my own eyes. The tenacity of nature!

In this chapter I have deliberately excluded badgers, which feature quite prominently in my work as a WLO. The next chapter is dedicated to them for this reason.

Badgers

As kingfishers are my favourite resident birds, badgers along with otters are my favourite mammals. Badgers are one of two British mammals that enjoy a special level of protection under British law, the other being bats. A great deal of my work as a police wildlife liaison officer is with badgers and, therefore, I have decided to devote this short chapter to them. Before I begin to relate some of the incidents involving badgers, I will attempt to give a résumé of their biology and legal protection.

The scientific name for a badger is *Meles meles* and they are members of the Mustelid family, which also includes the otter, stoat, weasel, mink, polecat and pine martin to list a few. With their black and white facial markings and dense grey coats, they are easily recognisable. Many books have been written about them, both fiction and non-fiction, and they have been immortalised in Kenneth Graham's *Wind in the Willows.*

Badgers are by classification carnivores but by habit they are omnivores. Their staple diet is worms, however, they will eat almost anything from roots to berries, baby rabbits to mice. They have been on earth for a long time, the first badger-like fossils have been found in Asian sediments dating back four million years. When fully grown they can measure one metre in length, and weights in excess of forty pounds have been recorded in road casualties. They are primarily nocturnal and very shy. The first encounter most people have with a badger is when they see one dead on the side of the road; indeed many landowners who have setts on their land have never seen a live badger.

Badgers are extremely powerful animals and expert exca-
vators, moving huge amounts of soil when digging their
setts. They have strong shoulder muscles and five long claws
on their mighty front paws. I have seen many setts where literally tons of soil have been dug out, and it is this activity
probably more than any other, which brings them into con-
flict with humans. Their digging activities are often very
conspicuous, which is in contradiction to their shy nature.
An active sett is quite distinctive, as there will be discharged
bedding near and around the sett entrance. This is one of the
first indications I look for when investigating a sett, for any
reason.

Badgers are sociable animals often living in large family
groups with some sett complexes being huge and extending
for long distances as generations of badgers have dispersed to
the edge of the site and dug new setts. I know of one sett that
extends over two hundred metres along a high-wooded bank
with a river flowing along the base of the bank. There are
over fifty sett entrances and, according to the farm records,
it has existed for well over one hundred years. Fortunately, it
is well away from any roads or footpaths and has remained
undisturbed. I have been very privileged to have the opportunity of both watching and photographing badgers at this
sett for a number of years.

As for longevity, badgers rarely live more than about ten
years in the wild, succumbing to disease or more likely the
roads. However, in captivity they can live up to twenty years.
They will use regular and well-worn tracks that have been
used by successive generations and, being somewhat stubborn animals, they will not deviate if a new road or housing
estate intrudes on to their track. They will often dig under
walls or smash through fences to continue along their path.

Their eyesight is abysmal, hence the reason why badgers
in fictional stories are often depicted wearing spectacles.
However, this is compensated for by excellent senses of

smell and hearing and, if attempting to watch badgers, you must always be down wind of them and you must also remain very quiet and still. As the first badger emerges from the sett, all you will see is the nose, which is scenting for danger. This procedure can take up to ten minutes before they are satisfied that it is safe to come out, and even then it is a very tentative movement. Normally once they have emerged, their first activity is to have a good scratch, sometimes leaning up against a tree before moving off to forage.

Amongst themselves, badgers are aggressive and argumentative; however, they appear to have a strict and complex social structure and order of dominance. In addition to having powerful front legs and claws, they also have very strong jaws, which will often inflict injuries during fights, normally between rival boars (males). It is this aggression that makes them attractive to the 'badger baiters' (I will explain more about this despicable activity later).

The dominant or alpha male will often force subordinate males from the sett, thereby ensuring that it will be *his* genes that are passed on to the next generation. Mating takes place soon after the sow has cubbed in January to February, but due to a process known as 'delayed implantation', the fertilised eggs will remain in suspension with very little development all through the following spring, summer and autumn. It is not until mid-December that the eggs will implant in the wall of the uterus and gestation begins. Two or three cubs are born after six or seven weeks. The sow is a devoted mother who will protect her young from all comers, whether it is a marauding boar (infanticide is not uncommon in badgers), a badger baiter's terrier, or a stray dog that might wander into the sett.

From late April to May, the cubs will emerge from the sett and it is this time of the year that is often the best time to watch them. On a warm still evening, sitting near a sett, you can be rewarded by one of the most extraordinary and wonderful sights in nature. The cubs tentatively emerge and start playing around the entrance, only to scuttle back into the safety of the sett as an owl hoots overhead or a muntjac deer barks. Both of these events have happened to me. At this age, the sow will often leave the cubs and forage for food for a short time. On one occasion I was sitting about fifty feet from the sett entrance when a sow passed within three feet of me. It was a wonderful moment.

Now that I have given a broad overview of the badger's biology, physiology and habits, I will turn to their legal protection. The law protecting badgers was introduced to curb the activities of the badger baiters and to stop the deliberate harm and injury caused to them. Not only are the badgers themselves protected but their setts are as well.

Badger-baiting is the pitting of a badger against a terrier and is termed by the baiters as 'sport'. The bait can take place at the sett where a badger will be dug out or by digging down to a point where the terrier can reach the badger in view of the baiters. Alternatively, the badger will be bundled into a sack and taken away to be baited elsewhere, usually in a pit. It would appear that the baiters like a suckling sow, as they put up the best fight while they try to protect their offspring. A fully grown badger can and will cause serious injury or death to a terrier, so it may be maimed in some way by either cutting off a front leg or by breaking the top jaw with a spade. Somehow the badger and terrier know that they can both cause horrendous injuries to each other with their jaws. I am often asked why badger-baiting takes place; I am afraid it is all down to money, as large bets are exchanged on the outcome. Alternatively, it is used as a method of training terriers to hunt, although I do not see the need as my Jack Russell terrier needs no encouragement. The courts take a very dim view of badger-baiting and prison sentences are often given out on conviction.

This brings me to the legal protection afforded to badgers. The activities of the baiters constitutes an offence by causing 'unnecessary suffering' under Section 1 of the Protection of Animals Act 1911. Although this is an old piece of legislation, it is the one most often used for offences of cruelty. The Wild Mammals (Protection) Act 1996 also specifies offences committed by baiters. Although these two enactments are very important, the major act specifically to protect badgers is the Protection of Badgers Act 1992. This superseded the Badgers Act 1973 and is the current legislation to protect them.

The Protection of Badgers Act 1992 creates offences as follows:

- Wilfully killing, injuring, taking, possessing or cruelly ill-treating a badger or attempting to do so
- Interfering with a sett by damaging it or destroying it
- Obstructing access to or any entrances of a badger sett
- Disturbing badgers when occupying a sett

As with any legislation there are exemptions, but the only one of any consequence, in my opinion, and the one that is continually tested, is the exemption offered to hunts and hunt servants who are permitted to 'stop' a sett prior to a hunt. This is to prevent the pursued fox taking refuge down a sett. The stopping of a sett is basically blocking the sett entrances with light material; and there are very strict guidelines in respect of this. If using soil it must be brought to the sett as they must not block the sett by collapsing the roof. After the hunt, the sett should be cleared. It is this exemption that is often a flashpoint at hunts, with allegations that the sett stopping is illegal due to the materials used or the amounts used. It is sometimes left for the courts to decide.

Now that you have an insight into the legislation afforded to badgers and their setts, I will now turn to a few experiences

I have had as a police wildlife liaison officer.

Soon after taking up this post, I was appointed as the police representative within the local badger protection group, the Uttlesford Badger Group, who are affiliated to the National Federation of Badger Groups. The Uttlesford group, like all the others, is made up of volunteers who do a tremendous job of protecting setts and caring for injured, sick or orphaned, badgers often under quite difficult conditions. Obviously the group is licensed by English Nature, as I am through the Essex Chief Constable, to carry out this work and not commit an offence under the act.

Shortly after joining the group, I was contacted one morning regarding an injured badger on the A120 at Takeley. I was due in court and therefore could not assist my two colleagues from Dunmow, who were trying to catch the animal that had run into dense bramble. Eventually, after numerous thorn scratches, they managed to catch the badger and place it in a hessian sack. The animal appeared to have a badly broken bottom jaw. She was handed to members of the badger group who had arrived just at the point of capture. She was conveyed to a vet in Saffron Walden, where she was sedated prior to a thorough examination. Badgers are difficult animals to handle at the best of times and injured ones are even worse. An X-ray revealed that the badger's bottom jaw was broken in five places and the vet was rather pessimistic but decided to carry out an exploratory operation while the animal was still sedated. This operation revealed that although it was a bad break it was repairable. With a lot of skill and dexterity, the vet managed to wire up the bottom jaw by splinting the broken bones. The badger was kept in for twenty-four hours and was then brought back to Thaxted, where the local badger group field officer, Dave Start, and his wife, Penny, lived. They had built a three-metre square wooden box with a roof and inspection cover, designed for the care of badgers.

The badger was an eighteen-month-old sow that Dave and Penny named 'Lucky'. Initially, she was fed on soft fruits, as eating was an obvious problem for her. Human contact was kept to a minimum and, as the days drifted into weeks, she made a rapid recovery. I took a series of photographs of her for the group and, after six weeks she was eating everything that was left for her. She was returned to the vet and sedated whilst an examination showed that the operation had been totally successful. The wire was removed and she was returned to Thaxted, where she remained for a further two weeks to recover fully from the effects of the anaesthetic. Then one wet and windy night, Lucky was taken to a stubble field near the sett where she had come from. The badger track that led to the sett and across the field was lit up. The box was opened and we waited for Lucky to emerge. She was apparently asleep in the box so we waited... and we waited. I began to wonder who had it right – she was nice and snug in her straw-lined box, while we were standing outside getting absolutely soaked and trying desperately to keep the cameras dry. There was a large group with us consisting of local media, members of the badger group and some other interested parties.

Eventually Lucky was persuaded to exit the box, albeit reluctantly. She shook herself and picked up the track immediately. She started to trot off along the track for about fifty metres, then stopped and turned her head to look at the assembled throng. It was as if she was saying thank you. She then ambled off out of sight and I think that everyone who had been involved had a lump in his or her throat. It was a credit to the work of the badger group and Dave and Penny in particular. After careful monitoring, it was later discovered that Lucky had cubbed the following year, which of course meant that she had been carrying the eggs at the time of the accident. The vet involved was presented with a framed photo of Lucky in recognition of the fact that he had not charged the group for her treatment.

One spring morning I was contacted by the field officer of the local badger group – the man who had reared Lucky back to health. A very distressed young lady had contacted him and reported that some six hours ago her Yorkshire terrier, by the name of Maxi, had disappeared down a large hole that she believed to be a badger sett. The dog had not come out and she and her husband wanted to dig down and try to get it out. In my role as WLO, I am licensed through the Essex Chief Constable and by English Nature to interfere with a sett in the course of investigating an offence. For a specific incident such as this, I would need an immediate licence issued by the Ministry of Agriculture to carry out any excavation work to rescue the dog. However, before such a licence would be issued, we had to be satisfied that the dog was still alive.

Dave and I went along to the sett, which consisted of twelve entrances at the top of a bank leading down to the River Chelmer. Dave was convinced that it was a nursery sett and it was absolutely silent. We spent the next two hours crawling around on all fours leaning deep into each of the sett entrances calling, 'Maxi, Maxi', but there was nothing. The couple were becoming more and more distressed. Eventually we all got to our feet and Dave and I shook our heads. The lady turned to us and asked in a tearful voice what we thought had happened to 'her little Maxi'. She was told that the badgers had probably eaten it. The couple then left; we had to tell them the truth. After the couple had left, I asked Dave how we were going to find out for definite what had happened to the dog. He replied that the collar would appear in the bedding in about ten days' time and, sure enough a tiny bloodstained collar with the small brass disc bearing the name Maxi was found. I did not return the collar to the couple. Under these circumstances we would not have been justified in applying for a licence to dig into the sett, as we could not establish that the dog was still alive.

Another evening I was on duty when I was sent to a local World War II airfield for a possible badger baiter. The airfield itself was criss-crossed with large concrete drainage tunnels and I was aware that badgers had taken up residence in at least two of them. At the entrance to one of the tunnels I found a man crouching with his head partially in the tunnel. As I approached him, he put his finger to his lips indicating for me to remain quiet and pointed to the tunnel. I quietly joined him and, without even putting my head into the tunnel, I could hear the sound of snoring coming from inside. It was really loud. We estimated that there must have been at least five badgers asleep in that particular tunnel, which was obviously well used by them, judging by the amount of bedding both along the tunnel and at the entrance. Their snoring was echoing and being amplified as the sound travelled along the concrete walls. The man walking past with his dog had heard the noise and decided quite innocently to climb down into the ditch to listen. I later learned that badgers can have bad sinuses, hence the snoring; and I have been trying to use the same excuse for myself ever since!

Early one morning I was called out from home to a local sett that had been extensively dug out overnight by badger baiters. The scene was one of total devastation. The amount of work that had been carried out suggested that there had been at least four people involved and they must have worked through the night. It was a large and well-established sett with numerous entrances, some of which had been blocked off with sharpened sticks to prevent the hapless badgers from escaping. At various locations the diggers had dug down at least ten feet to the main chambers. We made a thorough search of the site to try and find any clue to the identity of the diggers but there was nothing. There was no way of establishing how many badgers they had taken but, a few days later there were signs that the remaining badgers were trying to repair the damaged sett and we found fresh latrines. Unfortunately, we never did trace the people responsible.

Soon after this incident a local farmer discovered a very gruesome scene outside a sett on his land and contacted me. The sett was in a hedge not far from a road. At the sett entrance there was a heavily bloodstained snare that was held in place by a long steel peg. All around the snare were large pieces of badger flesh and hair and the grass was flattened and soaked in blood. A wider search revealed two sets of footprints in the damp soil, leading to and from the road to the sett and, more ominously, two sets of dog prints the size of which suggested terriers. At the road, there was mud that the two people had kicked off as they had got into a vehicle that had been parked in the field entrance a short distance away. The conclusion we reached was that the baiters had set the snare the night before, the badger had been caught and the baiters had returned and baited the creature with the two terriers while it was still in the snare. We did not find the carcass and I was curious as to why they had chosen to leave the snare behind. Again, I did not trace the people responsible, but I would like to have done.

On another occasion I was sent to Hatfield Forest, which is a large National Trust area near Stansted Airport, where a lady was reporting a suspicious incident that had occurred in the forest the previous day. She stated that she had been walking through the forest with a friend when they saw two men walking away from a car parked up in one of the many entrances to the forest. They were carrying something in a hessian sack and had two terriers with them. They disappeared into a dense part of the forest and the ladies thought they looked suspicious. As they hurried away, they heard dogs barking from the area where the men had disappeared. The ladies went home but decided to report the incident to the forest warden the following day. The warden and I went to the point described by the lady and, through some dense undergrowth, we reached a clearing with mature trees. Lying in the brown leaves was a dead adult badger. A shaft of sunlight was piercing through the bare trees on to the poor creature. It was obvious that it had been baited and this was confirmed by a post-mortem, which also revealed that it was a pregnant sow due to have three cubs about two weeks later. I was angry and frustrated. If only I could have caught the baiters!

One morning Dave brought a dead badger cub round to me. He had found it at a sett that he had been checking, around the entrance and down into the tunnel he had seen terrier and human footprints. A post-mortem was not necessary, as the cause of death was obvious. Badgers will sometimes kill their own cubs, usually a jealous boar, but in this case that theory was dismissed by the presence of the terrier tracks and the footprints.

During the early 1990s we experienced some very dry summers when worms, which are a badger's staple diet, tunnel deep down to avoid desiccation. They are out of reach for even the most determined badger. The lack of food forced badgers to forage during daylight hours and many cubs died of starvation. A lot of local farmers were reporting daytime sightings of badgers and, for some it was the first live sighting they had ever had. One such cub was found in the middle of a field and was so weak and emaciated that it gave little resistance when the farmer picked it up, although its needle-sharp teeth did draw blood. It was again cared for by

Dave and Penny who fed it on cat and dog food for two weeks. During this time it almost doubled its body weight and, once back to full health, it was transferred to a badger hospital in Somerset. Here, it was placed in a group of orphans of the same age and they were eventually released as a family group in an artificial sett at a secret location. A pair of orphaned cubs were reared in the same way and also went to Somerset for eventual release. These made the front page of the local press.

Another case that one of my WLO colleagues dealt with and with which I only had a very minor involvement was rather unusual. My colleague received an anonymous phone call to the effect that he might like to take a walk around a local car boot sale that was taking place on a disused airfield that day. Although we do not always act on anonymous information, he had been contacted in his WLO role and decided to take a look as his curiosity had got the better of him. On a stall towards the back of the sale, he found a man selling animal pelts. He claimed that they were racoon pelts but my colleague believed them to be from badgers. He pointed out that racoon stripes run across the animal's face and badger stripes run down the face. This argument was put to the stallholder who remained adamant that they were from a racoon. My colleague seized all twelve pelts and they were sent for forensic examination, which confirmed that they were all badgers of varying ages. The man appeared at the local magistrates court and was fined just over seven hundred pounds for possessing the pelts. It was never established where they had come from, although they were complete with no tears in them, suggesting they had not been baited. Road casualties were the most likely source. Obviously the man was not a naturalist, as he would have realised his mistake.

A particularly nasty incident of badger-baiting involved a lone brock badger that had dug a sett in a field of wheat, which was about three inches high. As usual the badger had not concealed its presence, which was its undoing. Sadly, someone had dug down with a spade (the marks were clearly visible) and managed to get the badger out. They then broke its top jaw with the spade, dragged it into a ditch nearby and killed it with terriers. It must have put up a tremendous fight, as there was blood everywhere. The animal was examined by a local vet who confirmed that he had died of multiple bites and that a sharp instrument, i.e. a spade, had broken its jaw. The curious aspect was that after it was killed the badger was thrown back into the sett, which was then filled in, only later to be discovered by the landowner who incidentally is a keen naturalist and was very upset at his find; as soon as he discovered the sett had been disturbed I was contacted.

A farmer friend once contacted me and asked me to have a look at a new pheasant-rearing pen that he had built in a local wood. Curious to see how he was going to keep foxes out, I agreed to have a look with him. The pen was about fifty feet square and was fine. He had placed a twelve-volt electric fence around the outside to keep the foxes out and this consisted of a single strand about nine inches from the ground. The only problem I could see was that he had placed the pen directly on top of a well-used badger run, which passed through the wood. I pointed this out to my friend but he dismissed my comment, saying that the electric fence would keep out all animals. My reply was, 'We shall see.'

About six weeks later my friend came roaring up to me one morning and demanded that I go and see what the b— badgers had done to the pen. Knowing full well what had happened, I went with him and, on arriving at the pen, the evidence was plain to see. The badgers had refused to deviate from their chosen route, one that they had probably used for time immemorial and had gone under the electric fence, their thick coats insulating them from the current. They had then literally barged through the wire fencing, leaving the characteristic inverted 'D' shaped hole. They had continued along their path and gone out the other side in the same way. The forty or so young pheasants had not been eaten by the badgers but had escaped only to fall prey to the fox. My friend was not happy and what he wanted to do to the badgers is not worth repeating. Of course, he was *only* joking, particularly as I warned him that I would have to prosecute him if he carried out his threat. (I was not joking!) The expression 'I told you so' comes to mind.

On the edge of the same wood, my Jack Russell terrier, Cassie, discovered a large wasps' nest in the ground and, although she made them angry, she did not get stung. It was a big nest and, about a month later, I discovered that the entire nest had been dug out. It soon became apparent by the claw marks that badgers had been at work. They were obviously after the big grubs within the nest, as it had been a very dry summer. Very few wasps had remained but a small piece of the nest of wood pulp was deep in the hole and it was apparent that the wasps were trying to rebuild it. Over the next few weeks the nest was rebuilt but the badgers played a waiting game and eventually returned to dig it out for a second time. On this occasion they totally destroyed it and the wasps did not return. It would appear that badgers are either impervious to wasp stings or they are not bothered by them.

As I have previously mentioned fox hunting has always caused problems for the police, with respect to badgers. A typical scenario arises time and time again and raises all manner of legal issues in respect of the actions of the hunt servants and the badger's act. The fox is flushed from cover and is pursued across fields by the hounds and the field.

Naturally, if a hole presents itself, the fox will take refuge there. These are often drainage pipes in ditches. The terrier man employed by the hunt is then deployed to flush the fox out using his terrier. This is often a flashpoint between the hunt and the antis. On some occasions, the terrier is retrieved from the pipe with horrific facial injuries due to a badger whose home it is, that has just been invaded. We then get all manner of allegations and legal arguments from badger group members and the antis. Violence often erupts and we have to move in.

Badgers show no respect to the dead of any species, including humans. The superintendent of a large cemetery once contacted me with his problem. A badger had dug into one of the large crypts and set up home. It was mid-February and it was likely to have been a nursing sow. There was a lot of fresh bedding at the entrance, including some bunches of flowers from the graves – obviously the sow had an eye for flower arranging and colour! The crypt was very old and the superintendent was happy to leave the badgers, which was just as well as we would have had difficulty in moving them. I had horrible visions of the badger cubs emerging from under the crypt with bones in their jaws. The superintendent later informed me that the sow and cubs had vacated the sett in autumn, which was a relief for everyone.

In November 1995 a local farmer contacted me. He had a problem with a large seventeenth-century Essex barn, which was a Grade II listed building. Essex County Council and English Heritage had visited him and advised him that he must bring the building up to standard as it was in a poor state. The barn was in fact sinking. The work to be carried out included the erecting of scaffolding, underpinning, repairing the bowed roof and to relath and plaster the external walls. You may be wondering why he contacted me. It transpired that the main reason the barn was sinking was that for the past fifty-odd years there had been a huge and well-established badger sett in the foundations of the barn and they had undermined it.

Dave from the local badger group and I visited the barn, as it was necessary for us to establish that the sett was in fact occupied before proceeding. There were eight main entrances to the sett and all of them disappeared under the barn. Two of them had fresh bedding outside and there were freshly used dung pits around and about. I then contacted English Nature for a licence to work on the sett. They visited the site and advised me that I would have to obtain a licence from the MAFF, as it was agricultural land. The MAFF representative then attended and informed me that, as it was technically a development, the licensing authority would have to be English Nature. Talk about red tape! While these two government bodies discussed the matter amongst themselves, the local badger group, the farmer and myself held a meeting to decide how we were going to proceed. The farmer was a keen naturalist and was initially reluctant to move the badgers, but it was pointed out that the work, particularly the underpinning, would interfere with the sett and would constitute an offence under the Protection of Badgers Act 1992. The farmer agreed for the group to build an artificial sett nearby and encourage the badgers to move. This would eventually be enforced with the use of one-way gates (I will describe those later).

English Nature eventually issued the licence to me and work commenced on the artificial sett. Local companies donated all the materials used. These included thick piping from a water company, sleepers from a coal merchant and six-foot long metal pins from a building supplier who also donated a roll of roofing felt. The group were very experienced at building artificial setts and this one was their eighth. The other seven setts were all happily occupied and we hoped that this one would work as well.

Work commenced in April 1996. Fortunately, one of the group's members owned a mini digger, which saved a lot of the back-breaking work. The plan was to run the pipe from an entrance under a tree, through a chamber built of sleepers bolted together and roofed with sleepers. A layer of roofing felt was added down the sides and over the roof to seal it and a concrete slab on the roof to protect it from farm machinery. It was unlikely that the machinery would reach this sett, as it was on the edge of a field and the tops of this and the second chamber were approximately four feet from the surface.

Pipes led out of the first chamber and into and out of the second before they exited out into a disused ditch a short distance away. Each chamber was capable of holding about thirty badgers, as it was estimated that there were up to forty badgers in the barn sett. The new sett was named the 'Badger Hilton' and we were considering putting lights on time switches for them, central heating, a sauna and a microwave but all they ended up with was some nice fresh dry bedding. This was in the form of straw and was placed in each chamber prior to the roof going on. The construction was completed and peanuts were scattered up the pipes and around the entrances to encourage the badgers to investigate their new home. Badgers love peanuts, particularly the sweet honey roasted form! A week later, Dave and I returned to find that all the peanuts had gone and there were distinctive badger pad marks up the pipes. This was excellent news, as they had obviously been into their new home. The badgers were then left alone throughout the summer to allow them to rear their cubs.

In early October of the same year, gates that reminded me of cat flaps based on a MAFF design were installed over each of the entrances to the barn sett. There were obvious signs that the badgers were in the 'Hilton', as bedding, including some of the straw that we had put in, was around both pipe entrances. Once the gates were in place, masonry was heaped around the sides and roof of each gate to prevent the badgers from digging around them. A few days later, there were signs that the majority of the badgers had taken the hint and moved to the 'Hilton'. We revisited the barn in mid-November and it was apparent by all the autumn leaves and debris around the gates that only one gate was now being used. This was probably by a stubborn old brock badger who was refusing to move. The eviction order was enforced by fixing a piece of wood on the outside of each gate, which would allow any remaining badgers out of the sett but not back in again. This worked and by Christmas of that year, the barn sett had been vacated and the 'Hilton' was fully booked.

A lot of work was done by a very dedicated team of people, concerned for the welfare of badgers and this resulted in a successful conclusion to the matter. Although there were some signs that one or two of the more stubborn customers at the 'Hilton' had tried to dig back under the barn, they had been unsuccessful and, once the worked started, we hoped that would be a sufficient deterrent! I took a series of photographs of the entire operation from the initial visit through to the completion of the 'Hilton', and now I give regular presentations on this matter under the title 'Badgers Undermining our English Heritage' which I think is rather apt.

Many years ago I was given a stuffed badger (sadly a road casualty) mounted on a board with grass and a log for realism. This badger was named Sid and came around with me on the ever-increasing number of talks I was asked to give to all manner of organisations such as schools, universities, social groups, colleges, camera clubs and the Women's Institute, to name but a few. Sid was very popular in the primary schools and the children loved to come and stroke him.

I remember one occasion when I was talking to a group of eight- and nine-year-olds on nocturnal animals. Sid featured prominently in the talk and the fact that he had been killed in a road accident enabled me to introduce the subject of crossing the road safely by using the 'Green Cross Code'. I told the children that poor old Sid had not used the Green Cross Code and that was why he was there as he was. A long pause followed as my comment sank in. Shortly a small hand went up at the back of the hall. I asked the little boy if he had a question and he came out with a real gem. He asked, 'Mr Wright, does that mean if I don't use the Green Cross Code, I will get stuffed like Sid?' The staff at the back of the hall exited with tears of laughter pouring down their cheeks and the other children were all giggling. For once I was lost for words – get out of that one!

With so many people stroking Sid, especially children, he inevitably went bald, and as you rarely get bald badgers in the wild, I had to retire him from the public speaking circuit. At about the same time, I was in a bar one night with a friend of mine and he happened to mention quite late in the evening that he had a badger in his freezer. I initially wondered what he had been drinking as I wanted some! It later transpired that he had killed the badger in a road accident in the lane leading to his farm. He was so upset that he had picked up the unlucky creature and placed it in his freezer, where it had lain for almost a year. I explained to him the plight of Sid and that I was looking for a replacement. He was over the moon, as the badger had not died in vain. He paid for the badger to be stuffed and mounted, which he felt was money well spent. The new badger was named Bert and is my present constant companion at the talks. I try and discourage both children and adults from stroking his head!

When I first started putting ideas and thoughts down for the foundations of this book, I was really struggling to find a title that would encompass its contents. Then one day I received a phone call from a colleague who said, 'Is that the "Wildlife Man"?' and in a flash I shouted, 'That's it, I've got it, I've got it, that's it.' My colleague was speechless on the other end and I think he thought I had finally gone round the bend. He had only rung me for advice on a badger issue. I have heard the term more and more from colleagues and members of the public and it therefore seemed a fitting and natural title for this book.

To conclude this chapter on badgers, I would like to relate two wonderful, memorable incidents involving badgers that I believe sum up these fascinating creatures.

The first took place late one summer evening. The sun had long set and stars were appearing in the early night sky as the light began to fade. I was out across the stubble fields with the two dogs, Chela, the black Labrador and Cassie, the Jack Russell. They enjoyed their evening walks to cool off after the heat of the day. Chela was racing off catching sticks that I would throw for her, while Cassie investigated all the scents in the stubble. The field had been combined that day and the air was full of the lovely scent of fresh straw, which is difficult to describe, but those who have experienced it will know what I mean. Chela had just returned with the stick and was waiting for me to throw it again. I swung my arm back and was about to hurl it into the field when I could not believe my eyes. There on the edge of the wood at the other side of the field, a large badger had appeared about two hundred yards from where I was standing. He was trotting quite nonchalantly along the edge of the wood on the headland between the stubble and the wood. It was obviously totally unaware of our presence and, as there was no breeze, it was unlikely to detect our scent. I very quietly placed both dogs on their leads and stood and watched the black and white form moving quite purposefully. It stopped once or twice, appearing to scent something on the ground. Fortunately, the dogs had not seen it and I was convinced that it would soon disappear back into the wood as quickly as it had appeared.

I watched in awe as the badger just kept going, still stopping from time to time. The moon was low on the horizon and was a deep orange – a harvest moon. Very quietly I moved along the footpath, parallel to the badger, as it approached the end of the wood and the open fields beyond. There was a ditch that separated the field that we were in from the one extending out of the wood. This ditch ran all the way along, passed two large oak trees to a second wood where my friend had previously placed his pheasant-rearing pen and where the wasps' nest had been dug up twice.

On reaching the end of the wood, I expected the badger to go back into it but he just carried on along the top of the ditch. What a wonderful sight it made as it drew level with that beautiful moon. I longed for my camera or someone to share the moment with. It is difficult to describe in words the beauty of the moment. The dogs remained oblivious to what was occurring on the other side of the field but were a little confused as to why they should have been placed on their leads in the middle of nowhere.

The badger continued on towards the second wood. He passed under the first oak tree but stopped at the second. He sniffed the ground and then appeared to dig a shallow hole and defecate into it. This was confirmed the following night when I investigated. These 'dung pits' or latrines are used mainly to mark out territories and is a method used by many animals. Having marked his spot, he continued and, as he drew level with the second wood, he disappeared into the dry ditch and emerged on the other side. A gentle mist was rising above the stubble as the badger entered the wood and was then out of sight. Was this the culprit who released the pheasants from their pen and destroyed the wasps' nest? I suspected that it was. The dogs were relieved to be let off their leads and I rushed back to tell Pat. It was difficult to describe, as I was so excited, like a child who has seen Father Christmas for the first time. I will never forget the moment when the badger drew level with that lovely moon – what a sight!

The second incident occurred in June 1995 on the South Downs and was one that I shared with Pat. We were on the Downs admiring and photographing some of the beautiful wild flowers, many of which were unique to the area. The wild orchids, in particular, held a special fascination for me. We had discovered a beautiful patch of fragrant orchids that were in full flower. It was a clear sunny day and the cotton wool clouds were scudding across the blue sky on a strong breeze. Skylarks were singing high above us and harebells fluttered within the grass. As we walked off along a well-worn path at the side of a hill, we stopped to photograph the slopes below us, which were ablaze with colour from buttercups, harebells, rock roses, daisies and orchids all in flower.

Pat suddenly grabbed my arm and said, 'Look, there's a badger,' and sure enough way down in the valley below us was an adult badger rummaging through the grass apparently looking for food. I just could not believe it. I quickly changed my camera lens from close-up to a long lens and started taking photographs. I was having difficulty holding the camera steady, so I used Pat's shoulder as a rest. It soon became clear that the badger was very slowly moving up the slope towards us. We intercepted a young couple and quietly showed them the badger but obviously they did not realise the significance of what was taking place, as they only watched for a few seconds before moving on. The fact that we were watching a mainly nocturnal animal, timid and shy by nature, without a care in the world, searching for food on a warm bright midsummer afternoon, was astonishing.

Several people walked past us unaware of the wonderful spectacle that was unfolding below us as the badger drew closer and closer.

After an hour of watching him and using a lot of film, I decided to creep very slowly down the slope towards the animal, which was by this time about one hundred yards below us. The slope was pretty steep, so in order to keep my balance I managed to move from anthill to anthill, as these gave me a purchase on the short grass. The breeze was in my face, so there was no fear of the badger picking up my scent or that of Pat who was moving down behind me. Also as the badger's eyesight is not good, we had luck on our side. In spite of this, I have to say I am surprised that the badger did not see me, as I was dressed in a brightly coloured T-shirt and pale jeans and my figure cutting the skyline was not small! We continued down the slope very slowly, as the badger continued up towards us. I was convinced that it was suddenly going to become aware of our presence and run off, but hunger and the search for food appeared to be the overwhelming thoughts on its mind.

Closer and closer we drew and I could not believe what I was seeing. I kept my movements as slow as possible, which was not easy on the slope and Pat had dropped back slightly but was still directly behind me. Eventually, to my amazement, the badger and I were less that ten feet apart. I had stopped photographing, as I thought that he might hear the electric motor on the camera, but also due to the fact that he was now too close for the focal length of the lens. I was not exactly in a position to change the lens, as it was as much as I could do to stay upright! I just stood and stared at this wonderful creature that was simply going about its business and was totally unaware of its audience. On one occasion it disturbed what I thought was a lizard or a mouse but Pat later told me that she thought it was a baby frog. Whatever it was it disappeared into a tussock of grass just as the badger pounced in an attempt to flush it out.

Suddenly with less than eight feet separating us, the badger ran towards me, chasing and catching a grasshopper. I was not breathing at this point but my heart was pounding. We were less than eighteen inches apart and I could have reached down and picked the badger up. It was absolutely incredible that even at that distance it still could not see me. The adrenalin was rushing and the hairs on the back of my neck were standing up. I dared not move a muscle, nor breathe. The badger pushed his snout into a tussock right on the end of my shoe and pulled out some grass by the roots with its teeth. It then did something quite curious. It laid the grass down and with its front paws started to rub the white parts of the grass stems towards the base against the ground. Was the badger cleaning the grass or tenderising the stems? I did not know but it soon proceeded to eat the white stems. I was witnessing something quite extraordinary – a wild creature in its natural environment within stroking distance. I had never seen a badger in broad daylight in the wild or so close. After eating some of the grass, the badger pushed his nose hard into the tussock at the end of my shoe for a second time. I thought he might hit my shoe but instead he brought out some insect, which he had already partially devoured as his head reappeared from the tussock.

We had been this close for what seemed like a lifetime, but in reality was about five minutes, when there was a momentary wind change as turbulence was created on the slope. The badger looked straight up at me, sniffed the air and then simply trotted off. He was quite unperturbed at picking up human scent and wandered off down the slope stopping once or twice to eat something before eventually disappearing into a thicket of yew. I took many deep breaths and looked at Pat who was as stunned as I was. It took me a few minutes to get my breath back and we were both speechless as we climbed back up the slope.

We sat down at the top of the slope and tried to take in what we had witnessed over the previous hour. I had gone through an entire reel of film but I did not know if they would all come out as I had had difficulty in steadying the camera in my excitement. Neither Pat nor I believe that we have ever experienced anything like that involving a wild animal before and would not expect to do so again. It was a truly magical moment and one to savour and cherish. It was a chance encounter that comes but once in a lifetime.

This last experience with a badger, which did result in some excellent photographs, leads me nicely into the final chapter of this book entitled 'Wildlife and Landscape Photography'.

Wildlife and Landscape Photography

I must emphasise at the outset of this chapter that I am not an expert photographer and, the views, ideas and techniques expressed are my own and not necessarily the accepted norm. I am self-taught and have had no formal training in photography; I probably know more about the subject that I am photographing than the equipment I am using.

My first camera was a very simple affair, which I won in a cereal packet competition. I can still recall it to this day on the back of the Shreddies' packet. All you had to do was to match the heads, feet and tails of various animals to their respective owners – I think there were six in total. It was during the mid-1950s and I was at Cheddington Primary School. I was so proud of this camera, which realistically was a fairly cheap example, taking 127-black and white type film – colour was still a long way off.

Not only do I remember the camera, but I also remember one of the first 'wildlife' pictures that I ever took. I was about eight at the time and it was a beautiful sunny day. Rex and I had gone off on a typical long walk, but this time I was proudly carrying my camera around my neck. We walked all along the railway embankment, past the village and then across the fields to Mentmore Park – a favourite place of ours. We were walking under the shade of the mighty horse chestnut and oak trees, when I suddenly found a dead jackdaw. It appeared to have died recently and was unmarked. Rex had a good sniff at it and ignored it. I picked it up, placed it on top of a nearby white sign and positioned it in such a way to make it appear alive, which was not easy! I took a series of photographs of it, which you may think was a macabre thing to do, but it was quite effective. The black and white photographs did not really do justice to the beautiful sheen of the dark feathers and grey head but I was still quite pleased with my first efforts, even if they were manufactured – I believe this is now know as 'Photographers' Licence'.

I continued my interest in photography at Jersey Zoo and I even acquired a new camera. Sadly, however, for whatever reason, I did not take a camera to France, which was regrettable. I compensated by buying postcards, which were stuck into the journal.

With joining the police service and a young family to keep me occupied, photography took a back seat for a while, but soon after moving to Thaxted I bought my first wife, Lyn, a camera, which we shared. It was a lot of fun, but with a fixed lens it had a very limited use for wildlife and close-up (macro) work. I bought my first serious camera from a friend who was upgrading her system. It was a single lens reflex camera or SLR for short. With the ability to interchange lenses from wide-angle to zoom or macro, this was the system that suited me. Over the years I have continued to upgrade my equipment and I now have an entire range of SLR cameras and lenses ranging from 1:1 macro to 500 mm zoom – a present total of fifteen lenses and six cameras. As you will see further on in this chapter, SLR cameras are in a world of their own for versatility, ease and speed of use, which are all essential components for wildlife photography.

I prefer to take transparencies (slides) mainly because I feel that this suits the saturation, depth and brilliance of the colours. There is a range of speeds of film in the 35 mm range to suit any type of photography. The slides are also easier to store and, as I have over nineteen thousand, storing and filing are important. The only down side is that it necessitates either a viewer or a projector and screen, unlike prints that are instantly viewable. My view is that if the photographs were worth taking in the first place, then the little effort to see them must also be worth it.

With wildlife photography, probably more than any other form, it is essential to protect your cameras and lenses when climbing through dense undergrowth or over rocks. One way to protect the lens is to fit an ultraviolet (UV) filter on the end. These cost very little but it is money well spent when you consider the cost of replacing the lens. As the name suggests, the filter will reduce the amount of ultraviolet light entering the lens and will counteract the problem of haze. I do not use any other form of filter.

Before moving on from cameras and lenses, the final piece of lens equipment, which I find essential for macro photography of flowers, insects or other close-up subjects, is a ring flash. This is simply a circular flash that fits on to the end of the lens and will compensate for the loss of light entering the lens due to the close proximity of the subject. Some really spectacular results can be achieved with this flash.

One final piece of equipment that is essential, particularly when using a long lens, is a rest in the form of a tripod or monopod. Personally, I prefer a monopod for fieldwork, mainly because it is more manoeuvrable and is lighter and less cumbersome. However, if shooting from a hide, a tripod is advantageous, as it means that you do not have to hold the camera all the time as with the monopod.

To illustrate the points I have just made, I will relate an amusing incident that happened to me a few years ago. I was on heathland in the south of England, attempting to photograph one of Britain's rarest resident birds, a Dartford warbler. I had located a particular flight path through a circle of gorse bushes that a specific male bird was using. He was landing on a small bush in the centre of the circle. I was using the 300 mm lens and set the camera up on the tripod with the lens pointed at the bush. Everything was focused and ready, I just had to wait. I was partly concealed behind a bush with a further bush behind me. A few minutes passed, when suddenly behind me I heard the sound of the warbler. I slowly turned my head to see the bird sitting less than four feet from me in the bush and in full view. Very slowly I tried to manoeuvre around the extended legs of the tripod slowly turning the camera on its swivel head, but of course the inevitable happened. Just as I was getting into position, the bird decided he had posed for long enough and flew off. I did eventually get a reasonable shot some time later using the monopod.

I think I have now covered most aspects of the equipment that I use, so I will now place my WLO hat back on to outline some legal aspects of wildlife photography, with particular reference to the restrictions on birds. Needless to say, the welfare of the subject should be of paramount importance to any photographer, and disturbance should be kept to a minimum. This is true in every case, whether the subject is a bird, mammal, reptile or other creature. If entering private land to photograph a subject, you must obviously ensure that you have the landowner's permission. If you are intending to photograph badgers at or near a sett, in addition to the landowner's consent, you must also inform the local Badger Protection Group, otherwise group members and police officers may descend upon you. Whilst mentioning badgers, I should remind you that the law protects the sett itself and therefore you must not position your camera or yourself too close, as it may constitute an offence of sett disturbance. Common sense should prevail. If bats are being photographed, the same rules apply, as their roost is also protected, even if it is your loft.

Rare breeding birds in the United Kingdom are protected when nesting by the Wildlife and Countryside Act 1981.

These birds appear on Schedule 1 of the act, which creates penalties for photographing these birds at or near their nest without a licence, issued by the appropriate authority. In England you should apply to English Nature, in Wales the Countryside Council, for Wales and in Scotland the Scottish Natural Heritage. Birds that currently appear on this schedule range from the avocet to the wryneck. A full list can be obtained from the RSPB.

Although there are no specific laws in respect of photographing other British wildlife, common sense must prevail when photographing any creature. One method that can be considered is the use of a small collapsible hide. This is particularly useful for birds who will soon get used to the new 'object' on their patch, and leads me nicely to an amusing incident that I had whilst photographing kingfishers.

For many years I had been trying to photograph kingfishers, which are my favourite British resident bird. They are shy, elusive and very quick, and pose a challenge to any serious photographer. They are given special protection under Schedule 1, so photographing them at or near their nest could land you in serious trouble. I would not want to risk a pair deserting their nest because of my desire for a perfect shot. With the loan of my father-in-law's small khaki canvas hide, I went to a river in Hampshire that I knew from previous visits was well populated with kingfishers, due to the large number of fish in the river. A particular post that leaned over the river was a favourite feeding post for these tiny birds to launch themselves into the water after their prey, which in this particular stretch of water was trout fry.

It was a beautiful clear sunny day with a gentle breeze and I set up the hide amongst a patch of stinging nettles to offer more cover. Once up, the hide stood about three feet high, so manoeuvring my six-foot high, large frame into the hide was not without its problems. Eventually I was in and perched upon a small folding three-legged stool I had brought with me. As I was lacing up the entrance, I heard the loud shrill call of a kingfisher as it flew along the river. It was a *cheeee* and *chikee*, the latter being the more common of its calls. I made myself comfortable and checked the camera set-up on the tripod. It was fitted with a 500 mm lens and a 200ASA film and I had to avoid the lens protruding from the hide, which was not easy. So with perfect conditions and the likelihood of the birds returning, I waited patiently. Sitting in a hide like this with the anticipation of not knowing what might appear outside is a very exhilarating experience for me. It gives me the same amount of pleasure as fishermen watching their floats.

The warm sunny day had brought out a number of inter-esting creatures, including some beautiful banded demoi-selle damselflies that were flitting over the surface of the water. They occasionally landed momentarily on the water crowfoot, its delicate white flowers just appearing above the water surface in the shallower parts of the river. A water vole 'plopped' into the water and swam directly towards the hide before disappearing under the surface, as the shadow of a magpie passed over the surface. The bird landed on a post on the opposite bank, where cattle were grazing. A large trout jumped clear of the water after a mayfly and re-entered the water with a loud splash, the water droplets glistening in the sunlight.

As I watched this idyllic scene, I became aware that the camera was becoming higher and that it was getting more difficult to see through the viewfinder. My little three-legged stool was slowly sinking and at the same time I had the most excruciating cramp in both legs. As I tried to straighten my legs, the movement on the stool caused it to sink even faster. I was in agony and hysterics at the same time, as I just could not lift myself up. The angle of my legs was wrong and I had nothing to take hold of to lift myself off the disappearing stool. While all of this was going on, a kingfisher had landed on the post immediately in front of the hide. I could see it through the flap in the hide but could not reach the eyepiece of the camera. Drastic action was needed and my only option was to fall sideways off the stool and then try to straighten my legs. So, still in hysterics, I carried out my plan and fell directly into the stinging nettles… ouch! I then lay down as best I could in this confined space and pushed my legs out of the back of the hide at the bottom so I could massage them. The cramp was a long time going but eventually I managed to sort myself out and by kneeling I could reach the eyepiece. To my absolute astonishment, the kingfisher was still on the post peering into the water, its iridescent blue green back shining in the brilliant sunshine. I released the shutter.

Over the next two days I took some excellent shots and achieved a lifetime's ambition. Equally important was the fact that the hide enabled me to watch wildlife at close quarters without any distress or alarm being caused. The kingfishers' themselves, provided some truly magical moments and an experience that I shall never forget. All the pain and discomfort was worth it.

With an opportunity such as this, it is, of course, essential that you have enough film with you, as there is nothing worse than running out at the crucial moment – the shot that you have been waiting for will always present itself when the camera is empty. Another point to remember, which is particularly relevant to wildlife photography, is to shoot when the subject and the opportunity are there. Never leave it thinking that a better shot may come along, as it may not and you will end up disappointed.

On another occasion, I was using the car as a hide on a riverbank in Cambridgeshire. A fellow photographer had informed me that a kingfisher would regularly perch on a strand of barbed wire which overhung the water to fish. It was a clear sunny day and the river surface was like a millpond. The bank opposite had been cleared of vegetation and was parched. The tall grasses and rosebay willow herb were full of common blue damselflies with their bright bodies shining in the sunlight, on the bank where I was parked.

Skylarks were singing high in the blue sky above me. I had been sitting there for over an hour when suddenly I heard a kingfisher calling from down the river with its unmistakable call. As it came closer, my body went rigid with anticipation and my finger was on the button ready to shoot but something appeared to be alarming the tiny bird that flashed past me and flew down the river, continually calling loudly *chikee, chikee*. My initial thoughts were that it was my presence that was bothering the bird, but all was soon revealed. A few minutes later, there was a *plop* in the water directly below me and ripples emanated from the bank edge. I thought that it was a fish jumping, as there were a lot of brown trout in this stretch of river, or that it was a water vole diving and the latter was strengthened by a line of bubbles floating to the surface in a line across the water.

Suddenly, a long black creature with a pointed nose and short tail emerged from the water on the opposite bank. Its wet coat glistened in the sunlight as it shook the water from its body. It was a mink. It ran up the bank and into the cover of the grass field, where it moved off towards a very old pollarded willow that overhung the river a little further along. I watched intently as it reached the tree and scaled its trunk with comparative ease. At this point, a pair of very angry magpies began mobbing the hunter with some ferocity. An avian predator attacking a mammalian predator is an uncanny irony. The magpies pressed home their attack as the mink entered the leaf canopy and disappeared from view. It did not remain in the tree for long and descended the trunk on the opposite side to me as, although I could not see it, the pursuers gave its presence away. Would you believe that in all the excitement I did not take one photograph? It was obviously the mink that had disturbed the kingfisher, which did not appear again that day.

I often say that with wildlife photography, probably more than any other form, it is a case of 'the five rights' which are:

- The right light
- The right place
- The right camera
- The right lens
- The right film

When all of these come together, the results can be perfect and the next few incidents will hopefully demonstrate what I mean.

To begin with, you do not need exotic locations for wildlife photography. Back gardens can host a myriad of wildlife. Our particular garden is not huge but we do have two ponds and the garden is bordered on all sides by tall shrubs and trees. This garden attracts numerous butterflies, dragonflies, frogs, toads and newts, as well as garden birds of all descriptions. The summer visitors include lesser spotted flycatchers and garden warblers, whilst swallows, swifts and house martins feed on the insects in the air above the garden. Some of the experiences in this garden I would like to relate in the next few paragraphs.

Early one summer morning, Pat and I were sitting in the garden having breakfast when we saw a speckled wood butterfly flying around the open flower of an osteospermum. I fetched the camera just as the butterfly landed on the central part of the flower and remained there long enough to obtain two good shots of it. With the red fuchsias in the foreground, the end result was an excellent shot.

Another warm still summer day I was sitting in the garden near the ponds working on my next assignment for my Open University course but being distracted by the activity in and around the ponds. Suddenly, a magnificent large dragonfly appeared above the surface of the water and hovered as it searched for food in the bushes behind the pond. Its yellow and black striped body with its huge wings shone in the sunshine. I continued writing when I suddenly became aware of something humming ahead of me. I looked up to see the dragonfly hovering about eighteen inches from my face and staring straight at me. We looked at each other for several seconds before it decided that maybe I was bit too big to tackle and it flew off back to the ponds. A few minutes later the dragonfly was hunting through the tree behind me when a white butterfly appeared over the garden about twenty feet in the air above the lawn. The dragonfly buzzed past my ear and flew fast and low, just above the grass before suddenly going vertical like a fighter aircraft. It came up underneath the butterfly and hit it. The hunter and its hapless prey drifted down on to the lawn. I went over to investigate, thinking that the dragonfly would fly off with its catch as I approached, but to my surprise it remained on the grass intent on eating its prey. I grabbed the camera and lay down on the grass. I crept towards the insect that continued eating and managed to take some good shots. Macabre you may think, but it is nature in the raw and quite fascinating.

Another time Pat and I were sitting in the garden on an August evening. We were watching the aerial exploits of the swifts with their young when a hummingbird hawk moth suddenly appeared from nowhere and began hovering around the hanging baskets and feeding from the geranium flowers. It would hover in front of the flower and its long tongue would go down into the flower feeding on the nectar. Its wings were beating so fast that they were a blur. The insect would then move sideways to the next flower. I fetched the camera and, as the light was fading, the flash as well. I was using a 400ASA film and, although I took some nice shots, the film coupled with the flash did not freeze the wing beat as I had expected. It was a fascinating insect to watch, though.

Gardens can provide some excellent photo opportunities, but always ensure that there is a film loaded in the camera in anticipation of the unexpected!

To visit a seabird colony in the height of the breeding season is a must for any serious bird photographer. Pat and I visited the Fame Islands off the Northumberland coast in June, and what an experience that was. This particular year, there were an estimated one hundred and seventy-five thousand pairs of birds on two of the islands that we were allowed to visit. This figure included a staggering thirty-five thousand pairs of puffins – one of my favourite auks. Other birds included razorbills, cormorants, guillemots, kittiwakes, eiders and fulmars. As we arrived on the first island in the small fishing boat, we saw birds everywhere, in the water, flying around the boat and all over the cliffs. I had brought six reels of film with me and was concerned that I may not have enough! I was using three cameras and Pat carried the lenses in a rucksack. I was so excited that I nearly fell off the boat as we disembarked. The air was full of the smell of ammonia from the guano and the noise was incredible.

With the birds having little fear of humans, it was possible to get quite close to them, so I had to change lenses from long to wide-angle. Puffins were flying overhead returning to their burrows with beaks full of sand eels. On one occasion, a puffin came in being mobbed by a gull, which was trying to force it to drop the fish in its beak. In attempting to avoid the gull's attentions, the puffin missed its burrow, swung around and landed on a rock in front of us. With the sun behind the bird, it shone through the almost transparent sand eels and made a good shot. The gull had broken off the attack. Everywhere we looked there was a frenzy of activity. The birds that had not hatched off their young were sitting tight. We watched a cormorant sitting on a nest about two feet from the walkway. It was panting in the bright sunlight, but as we watched, we suddenly saw a tiny little, wet head appear from under her chest – the chick had literally just hatched. Immediately adjacent to another walkway, a female eider duck was sitting tight on a nest. Her brown striped plumage provided perfect camouflage and she was really difficult to spot. Another eider had nested under an elevated section of walkway and was completely unperturbed by people walking over her. We spent two glorious hours on this island, which was the maximum we were allowed to stay, primarily to avoid causing the birds any undue stress. There were twelve people in our group and we all boarded the boat to visit the second island.

The warden met us as we landed on this island and advised everyone to put on hats or cover their heads, as the terns would attack. Pat used the hood of her waxed jacket and I had my flat cap on anyway. There was one gentleman on the boat who dismissed the warden's advice with an arrogant wave. Within a short distance of the boat, his bald head was bleeding where a tern had pecked him – the warden was not wearing a green hard hat for no reason! I photographed an arctic tern, more puffins and a beautiful pair of fulmars, which I found on a grass bank with a ledge about eye level. One of the fulmars was sitting on an egg and the mate was nearby. Just at this moment, the same gentleman joined us. I had taken the shot that I wanted, whilst keeping my distance and avoiding their defence strategy of 'spitting'. However, the gentleman decided that he wanted to get in closer. I warned him of the possible consequences but he dismissed my friendly advice with the same wave of the hand that he had given the warden. Closer and closer he went and it was obvious to any ornithologist that the birds were becoming a little agitated. Suddenly, as if synchronised, both birds let forth a shower of green, foul-smelling liquid with great accuracy. Both he and his camera were covered. He walked off in disgust as Pat and I could hardly hold back our amusement. The birds settled back down and we walked off to the old lighthouse building where we sat on a bench and had our picnic. All of a sudden a 'splat' of bird muck hit the rucksack. We looked up to see the rear ends of five puffins over the top of the white wall behind us. They were about ten feet up and it would have made a good photograph, but as I reached for the camera, they flew off. On the boat back to Seahouses, the gentleman was still covered in the green fluid and was rather smelly. He sat on his own. So ended a truly remarkable day and one that Pat and I will never forget.

Whilst on the subject of fulmars, another interesting photo opportunity presented itself while I was on a residential school trip to the Isle of Wight a few years ago. I was up and about early one morning before any of the children or staff had emerged and I crept out with my camera to go for a walk along the beach at Sandown. High sandy cliffs overlooked the beach and I soon became aware that there was a breeding colony of fulmars at the top, which was totally inaccessible. I watched the birds gliding in fast along the face of the cliff and then swooping up to the nest site. I tried to photograph the birds in flight by shooting as soon as they entered the frame of the lens, but that did not work. I then tried another technique – trying to follow the birds along the cliff face, matching their speed and shooting on rapid fire on the camera. This is probably the most expensive form of photography with a reel of film passing through the camera in less than thirty seconds. I had a lot of heads and tails but in amongst the shots were two almost perfect pictures with the birds dead centre frame and the cliff face out of focus as a blur. This gave the effect of speed, which would not have been achieved if the photograph had been taken with a stationary camera.

Remaining with the water theme, another bird that I enjoy photographing is the swan, particularly the beautiful and graceful mute swan. The females or pens with young can become particularly aggressive as they protect them. The males or cobs in particular are the ones to watch. I was photographing a lovely family group consisting of a cob, a pen and four cygnets when the cob moved away and started coming towards me. As he did so, his wings started to rise on his back – that is the first threat. The second is a loud hiss and, if you can hear that, then you are too close. The third is too late as they suddenly rush at you with wings extended. All three happened to me on this occasion and I was only saved by the tall undergrowth between a very angry cob and myself. As I retreated, he returned to his family with his head held high in victory!

On another occasion I was in a deep reed bed trying to photograph the reed warbler. It was a lovely sunny day and the early morning mist was just lifting when I saw a pair of mute swans flying through the mist in the distance. As they approached me, they began to bank around towards an expanse of open water. Using the same technique that I used with the fulmar on the Isle of Wight, I followed them around with the camera but this time with a long 500 mm lens, which made it that much harder. The end result was one excellent shot with the swans in focus and the background trees in a blur. The picture looks, so I was once told, like a painting – I had never thought of myself as an artist!

I was sitting in a hide one winter's morning overlooking a lake. It was a bright sunny day but the lake was partially frozen over. I was not looking for anything in particular but there was a notice in the hide suggesting that kingfishers can often be seen perching on one of the two stumps sticking out of the water immediately in front of the hide. The surface of the lake that was not frozen over was like a millpond and was

213

giving a clear reflection of the tall overhanging willow and alder trees on the opposite bank. After almost five hours in the hide, very little had happened and I was about to leave when a large flock of black-headed gulls appeared from over the trees and began to fly low over the water. There were about fifty in the flock in their winter plumage of all white with a black spot behind the eye. They were shining in the bright sunlight, when suddenly they all banked around in one synchronised motion and began to circle just above the water's surface, as if on a thermal. I took a few shots just for fun with a fairly fast film and was quite surprised when the slides were returned. One shot in particular showed all the birds with the wings on each in different positions – an excellent example of 'flight' – which is what we have entitled the resulting print. It just goes to show that a bit of fun with a camera can end in unexpected results.

One Mothering Sunday, I was on Worthing seafront with my mother, walking off a fairly heavy lunch. The sun was setting behind the pier and I took a couple of shots with the red sun through the pier supports and reflected off the wet sand, as the tide was out. We then walked up on to the pier. The sun was slowly setting behind layered cloud above the horizon and casting a beautiful red glow over the empty beach, show-ing the empty ripples of the receding tide. The camera was active again, the sunset looked quite spectacular and there were a lot of like-minded photographers on the pier that evening. When the slides were produced, one particular shot that had been totally unexpected was the setting sun and the beach with five seagulls flying across the sun in silhouette. That really made the picture and I had not seen them in the frame when I took the shot. It made mother an excellent Christmas present the following December!

Butterflies and moths make interesting and challenging subjects on warm sunny days as they become very active and can be difficult to shoot. I have already mentioned the speckled wood butterfly in our garden. Skipper butterflies are mainly insects of open grassland and clover beds. We are lucky to have three fields behind our house with uncultivated grassland and scrub that have been left for at least fifteen years. In high summer, skippers appear in their hundreds but are difficult to photograph because of their skittish behaviour. One morning I found a pair mating on a grass stem next to a path regularly used by dog walkers. I lay down and proceeded to photograph the pair when suddenly I became aware of something out of my right eye. There was a little old lady standing next to me with a Yorkshire terrier who was eyeing me with curiosity. I smiled and said, 'Good morning', but she just gave me a filthy look and walked off with a disgusted look on her face. I think she thought I was some kind of pervert!

A similar incident occurred one morning when I received a phone call from a lady to say that she had two 'monsters' on her clothesline post and asking me to help. With camera in hand I attended the house, which was not far from us. I had a suspicion that I knew what it was but was not certain at this stage. Sure enough it was a pair of privet hawk moths mating. I took a series of photographs, much to the disgust of the lady concerned, before I gently removed them out of her garden. It turned out that she had a real phobia about moths and it was as if they seemed to know this as the incident was repeated the following year.

The months of May and June are often good months to find hawk moths resting during the day in fairly exposed places. These provide excellent photographic opportunities and even some macro shots. The resting insects are normally females, which although resting, are in fact sending out pheromones for the males to find them. A male within three miles of the female can pick up these chemical messages.

The following night the male comes in and takes her away on 'honeymoon'. I have seen and photographed the elephant hawk moth, privet hawk moth, poplar hawk moth, white ermine and, in Jersey the huge convolvulus hawk moth, which is an impressive creature with the largest wingspan of any British insect at three and a half inches (90 mm). As a footnote, unless the creature is in immediate danger, you are advised not to move them as they have chosen that particular spot for a reason. This really applies to all creatures.

Wild flowers are popular subjects for photography, often giving as much fun finding them as shooting them. They range from the early spring flowers such as the wood anemones, violets, arum lily, cowslip and oxlip, to the wild orchids in which I am particularly interested. There are over fifty species of wild orchids in Great Britain and I have so far been able to photograph twelve, so I have a long way to go. As a warden of a small wild flower meadow nature reserve owned by Essex Wildlife Trust, I have an ideal opportunity for flower and other wildlife photography. I take many groups around this reserve and often cringe as I watch some of them trampling down flowers in their eagerness to take a perfect photograph. I would rather miss the shot than destroy anything. Another point to remember is that if you are taking close-up shots, a flash may be needed to compensate for the loss of light. This is where a ring flash becomes useful as previously mentioned.

I was visiting a friend's wild flower meadow one sunny June day and there were butterflies and insects everywhere. The skylarks filled the air with song and it was a perfect day for photography. On the edge of the field was a patch of teasels that were in flower and attracting a lot of insects, mainly bees. Suddenly I noticed a beautiful brimstone butterfly feeding, her brilliant yellow wings almost luminescent in the sunlight. It was flitting from flower head to flower head as I followed it. Eventually my patience was rewarded and I took a lovely shot with the sun shining through its wings, silhouetting its body. These butterflies are unlike all others found in this country, as they never appear to bask in the sunlight with their wings open. Others do this to concentrate sun on to their bodies but the brimstone does not have the need to.

At one time Pat and I were photographing the very rare lizard orchid, one of Britain's rarest, and were getting some excellent shots, when Pat found a small white pupae on a grass stem and the insect within was just emerging. It was a seven spot burnet moth. Fortunately, Pat was carrying my spare cameras, including one with a close-up lens, which I used to photograph the process. It was difficult to keep the grass stem still in the strong breeze but I eventually managed to take a good shot. Although burnet moths are not particularly unusual grassland insects, to see them at the point of emerging from their pupae is a rare sight.

Whilst in the Water Meadows at Winchester one summer, I was trying to photograph a water vole, a species that is becoming increasingly rare in Britain, primarily due to predators such as mink as well as loss of habitat. I had been there all day without success and the setting sun bathed the meadows with an orange glow. I was about to leave when I caught sight of a magnificent roe buck standing under some trees at the edge of a dense reed bed on the opposite side to me of one of the many wide streams that intersect these meadows. I ducked down behind the reeds in front of me and crept towards the deer changing lenses as I went. This is not the easiest of tasks when one is virtually on all fours! When I considered that I was as close as I thought I was going to get, I slowly raised my head and was pleased to see he was still there. He was about two hundred yards from where I was hiding, looking directly at me in the fading sunlight. I took one shot and went for a second but he was gone. He had heard the camera even at that distance – oh, for a silent camera! The following autumn I was in the same location, still trying to obtain a good shot of a water vole and was in the process of packing up at the end of the day. I had not taken a single shot, which is very rare for me, when suddenly I spotted a fox hunting on the edge of the reed bed ahead of me. Again I took one shot and he was gone. The roe deer shot came out well and was improved by the beautiful sunlight but the fox shot was not the best, as it was quite a distance away and not really clear in the resulting slide.

One fallow deer that I did get some lovely shots of was a young doe by the name of Hazel who was hand reared from about twelve days old. She had been in a road accident and had sustained a fractured skull. A colleague of mine, Trevor Bailey, reared her with two-hourly feeds day and night for three months. Luckily, she survived and thrived. Pat and I first met her one evening when she was about eighteen months old. She was hand tame and beautiful. I had taken my cameras and shot some lovely pictures including a series of Hazel taking carrots very gently from Pat's teeth. Hazel eventually grew too big for Trevor's garden and joined a small fallow deer herd at Stansted Mountfitchet Castle, where they are on view in beautiful surroundings.

Remaining with deer, I had always wanted to visit Scotland during the red deer rut. This is normally in October and it is the time when the magnificent red stags with their huge antlers do battle with rivals as they try to gather up their females (hinds) into harems. Although I had watched it in films, I had never heard or seen it in the natural state. Pat and I had visited Scotland on a number of occasions, including on our honeymoon, and a few years ago we spent two weeks touring in October, which we had not done before. It was cold and there was snow on the mountains in the highlands. The scenery was quite spectacular and driving up into the mountains we soon discovered what we were looking for. The first time that I heard the roar of the stag, it sent a shudder down my spine and made the hairs on the back of my neck stand up. It was a truly primeval sound as it echoed down the valleys. It is one that I will never forget and has been known to carry for miles. The stags are so preoccupied with the rut and mating with as many hinds as possible, that they take very little notice of human activity. Using the car as a hide, I took some wonderful shots, particularly with the 500 mm lens resting on the open window. A terrific fortnight not only with the red deer but also photographing pine martins, crested tits, capercaillie red squirrels and wolves. It was an expensive holiday on film but worth it. The red deer rut is a must for any serious wildlife photographer.

Staying with the theme of wild open places, the heather moorlands of Northumberland are where we discovered red grouse and the fact that they can be quite inquisitive. One cock bird, in particular, was standing his ground near to where the car was parked. To try and take a closer shot, I crept around and on to the heather about fifty yards from the bird that was watching me intently. I then lay down on the heather and took a couple of shots with the long lens, as it was a lovely sunny day and the light was excellent. As I lay there, the bird started walking slowly towards me in a type of zigzag across the frame of the camera. I kept completely still. As the bird was getting nearer and nearer to me, it appeared to be going further down into the heather. The minimum focal length of the lens I was using was about nine feet and the bird had reached that. However, it had all but disappeared from view, so with some difficulty, I managed to roll on to my side and change the lens for another that I had in my pocket. Almost immediately after the bird bobbed his head up less than four feet from me, I took two shots. The bird had seen enough and flew off, I was so close that I felt the wind from his wings – who needs a hide?

A similar incident occurred on Winchester Hill in Hampshire and involved two different species of birds. The first was a yellowhammer that was sitting on a young ash tree singing its distinctive tune that is often likened to 'A little bit of bread and no cheese'. With the long lens on, I very slowly approached, keeping my body completely still and only moving my feet inches at a time. The bird appeared to be unperturbed by my presence and I crept closer until I was less than ten feet from him. He was singing his little heart out and did not stir even when I had to change film. Unbeknown to me, Pat was capturing me on film taking pictures of the bird.

The second bird was a willow warbler that was perched at the top of a hawthorn bush singing its beautiful transcending song. As I crept towards him, he looked straight at me and I thought he was going to fly but he continued to sing. Again I managed to get within ten feet of it and, I think the secret is not to make any sudden movements. Your feet have to move at a snail's pace.

Photographing otters creates its own challenges; the primary one is finding them. For many years they were extinct in East Anglia but through the wonderful work of the Otter Trust, a release programme over many years throughout the region has given these lovely animals a foothold. A lot of time and patience is required along with stout waterproofs and immunity to midge bites.

I once stood in a reed bed in deep water waiting for an otter to return to its holt built in the base of a willow tree. The tree overhung the water about two hundred yards from where I was standing. It was hot and muggy and during the course of the day I was ravaged by biting midges, their target being my hands, neck, face and head. By the end of the day I was covered – it brought back memories of the south of France. As the sun was setting, I was about to pack up when suddenly without warning the otter climbed out of the water and into the tree. I took a picture as she emerged and she obviously heard the camera as she turned in my direction, but being unable to pinpoint where the sound came from, she disappeared into the bowels of the tree. She came out again a few moments later and rested her head on a bough of the tree as the sun set. It was a lovely moment and even the midge bites were well worth it.

Remaining with the water theme, the rich diversity of wildfowl and other water birds in Great Britain offers some excellent photographic opportunities. During the mid-1980s, Lyn and I had a small cottage on the north Norfolk coast near Wells Next The Sea. During the winter months, huge flocks of brent and pink-foot geese would descend on the area from northern latitudes to feed and roost in a comparatively warmer climate than that which they had left behind. I have lasting memories of these huge flocks lifting off the fields in the fading winter light, silhouetted against the red sky. It is one of the many wonders of nature that make the hairs on the back of your neck stand up. It is no wonder that Sir Peter Scott derived so much pleasure from watching and painting wildfowl in its natural environment. The sight alone is quite spectacular and, in addition, you hear the sound of the flocks with their deep honking call that pierces the silence. As well as the geese, small flocks of ducks such as wigeon and teal used to circle around in the evening sky particularly in the marshes and reed beds along that stretch of coastline. I regularly visited Cley and Salthouse to listen to the haunting call of the curlews as they flew overhead and inland to roost. Altogether, the area is wonderful and another place to recommend for wildlife photographers.

The various reserves and visitor centres operated by the Wildfowl and Wetland Trust (WWT) also offer excellent opportunities for photography. With localities throughout the United Kingdom, the variety of species is endless, whatever the time of year. The centre at Arundel in Sussex has provided me with some wonderful photographs, but one particularly memorable one involved a pair of goldeneye ducks.

The drake is very handsome with beautiful black and white plumage and, of course, the bright yellow eye. The female is typically brown and drab in colour. It was early in the year and pairing, mating and nesting were in full swing. The drakes were showing off to the females by swimming along, then suddenly throwing their heads on to their backs, beaks pointing towards the sky and kicking out with their webbed feet in the water. They created quite a splash as they powered along like an outboard engine on a boat. With a fairly fast film and good light, some nice effects can be achieved with the water. However, this tiny little duck has a much more interesting trick up its sleeve and it is one that I have never seen performed by any other species of duck. Both male and female will regularly swim on their backs. One female I photographed was swimming leisurely in this fashion, with one foot up out of the water and the other gently paddling, causing her to drift in circles. A male I photographed was not only swimming along on his back but actually asleep with his head buried in his chest feathers. I would not have believed it had I not seen it and taken photographic evidence.

Although not native to Great Britain, mandarin and carolina wood ducks are now found almost all over the country as the feral population increases and spreads. Their brightly coloured plumage makes them very photogenic. One of my favourite duck species in addition to the goldeneye is the diminutive smew that is a winter visitor to England from northern Scandinavia and Russia. The male is a very handsome black and white, whilst the female has a lovely brown cap. The smew is a sawbill feeding on fish and shellfish and is a challenging bird to photograph as it continually dives for food. I have wasted a lot of film taking shots that later show ripples of water and no duck, due to the fact that it dived just as I pressed the shutter. However, patience and a lot of film will be rewarded eventually! This also applies to the little grebe (dabchicks) and great crested grebe that also spend a lot of their lives under water.

The courtship display of the great crested grebe is one of the most beautiful sights on an English lake in the spring. The pair will reaffirm their bond in a most elaborate way. After swimming apart for some distance, they will turn and race towards each other with necks extended and lowered just above the surface of the water. On meeting they will rise up, stand on the water and bob their heads from side to side, often with weed hanging from their beaks. It is a very graceful dance and worth capturing on film.

There are many other subjects that I have photographed, but I believe that the previous pages have given an insight into some of the wonderful photographic opportunities that British wildlife can offer. I will now turn to landscape photography, which is another passion of mine.

Any rural landscape and the moods of nature all through the year seem worth capturing on film to me. With good light, a slower speed film can be used, which will result in the picture having a much finer grain. Personally, I love the uncultivated moor and mountains and have been fortunate enough to visit many wild and beautiful parts of England and Wales on residential school trips over the years. Places I have stayed at include North Yorkshire, Snowdonia, the Lake District and the Peak District, and these untamed regions offer some splendid landscape photography with the light and weather constantly changing. Waterproof clothing and covers for the cameras are essential and I recall a classic situation on the climb up Mount Snowdon. As we left the base, it was with clear blue skies above and the sunshine was quite warm, but halfway up the mist began rolling in creating a lovely effect as it reached across the hills and down into the valleys. By the time we had reached the peak, it was raining hard but fortunately we were all prepared for it.

One of my favourite spots and one that I have visited several times with schools is Aysgarth Falls in the National Park in North Yorkshire. With shallow waterfalls stretching for over a quarter of a mile through a tree-lined valley, the photography is excellent. There is also the bonus of dippers, kingfishers, yellow and grey wagtails, buzzards and herons, plus the very diverse plant life in amongst the trees, which includes wild garlic. It is a truly magical place.

You may watch the dippers bobbing on a stone in the middle of the river, then suddenly diving under the water, only to reappear shortly afterwards further upstream with a beak full of insects. This is fascinating enough in itself but then these lovely little birds, about the size of a blackbird, perform a feat that to me is quite incredible.

They will fly low to the water surface and, on reaching the waterfall, they will fly straight through the curtain of water to their nest behind. They reappear shortly afterwards, having fed their fledglings either in the nest or perched on a mossy rock behind the waterfall. It is quite remarkable.

It was during one of these trips to Aysgarth that we went out in the coach to the Buttertubs Pass in Swaledale and climbed the hill behind the Buttertubs themselves. The view down into the valley was spectacular and was accentuated by the shadow of the clouds as they passed across the sun – my camera was busy. Many years later, this landscape photograph was the first that I ever sold (more on that later).

Whilst on another school trip to a hostel in Capel Curig in Snowdonia, we had a lot of opportunities to photograph rainbows, which created some excellent shots with the backdrop of the mountains. It was as we were staying at this hostel that I had an amusing incident with what I thought was a curlew.

My room had a panoramic view of a valley leading up to a spectacular peak and to the right of my window was a tall pine. I awoke early one morning before any of the children had stirred and this was a feat in itself. I could hear a curlew calling outside and it appeared to be close to my window. I had been trying for many years without success to photograph these wonderful birds with their long curling beaks and brown mottled plumage and I prepared my camera for action. I put on a long lens and very slowly opened the curtain a fraction. The sun was already up and the newborn lambs on the moor beyond the hostel were bleating. Still the curlew was calling but I could not see it. I scanned the ground with my binoculars but saw nothing. I was becoming perplexed as I could hear the bird but there was no sign of it. Again I combed the ground outside and became more mystified. I began to realise that the sound was coming from the tree, which confused me totally as curlews do not perch in trees. Then all became clear – sitting right at the top of the tree was a starling and it was mimicking a curlew perfectly! I shot some lovely landscapes instead.

Snowfall on a landscape can result in some stunning shots. I remember attending a summer school on my Open University studies at Malham Field Study Centre, Malham Beck, North Yorkshire. It was April and cold at night but warm and sunny during the day. At 5 p.m. on the second evening, we had a tremendous snowstorm, which continued well into the night. The following morning the landscape was transformed into a white desert, the blue sky was reflected in the still surface of the tarn and made a wonderful photo opportunity. Later that day, as I watched the large flakes falling again, a wonderful sight unfolded as two swallows flew through the snow towards me and over the centre – what a photo that would have been!

Sunsets have always been a favourite of mine for photography. Whilst in Jersey, I had always wanted to shoot the often spectacular sunsets at Corbière Lighthouse on the western end of the island but I never did. However, Pat and I were visiting a few years ago just before Christmas and one day there was a clear blue sky so we decided to try and see the sunset. We had a real treat in store. As the sun set, the sky turned red and I took two shots from the causeway to the lighthouse. With the sun setting between the rocks, the light formed a star effect in one shot that, although unexpected, made the shot perfect when the slides were developed. Back up on the rocks above the lighthouse, the sea was also red as it reflected the sky and this provided more excellent shots. It was well worth braving the bitterly cold wind, although Pat might not agree! It snowed the following day, which is a rare occurrence on the island.

Storms and rainbows, particularly over moors and mountains, can be great fun and can turn up some unexpected results. Pat and I were driving back through Allendale from Ullswater one summer evening and a storm had passed over us. As the cloud cleared the horizon, the setting sun burst through and the light was fantastic. One particular shot was of some sheep in a valley extending away from the road where we were sitting. The sheep were casting long shadows from the low sun with the dark sky above them and the landscape beyond them bathed in a yellow glow – the overall effect was wonderful.

As with wildlife photography, landscape photography is also subject to 'the five rights' and, when they all come together, the results can be very good. This was further highlighted one snowy winter morning when I was driving to work. The sky was overcast and began to glow red in the early morning light. As it grew more and more red, I stopped the car and took out my camera. The low cloud was glowing in layered bright crimson and with bare trees silhouetted on the horizon, the effect was quite spectacular. As soon as the sun broke the horizon, the red disappeared as fast as it had arrived and, contrary to the rhyme, it did not snow or rain that day. I was later accused of using a red filter to get such an effect, as people are convinced that sky is never that colour. However, I do not even own a red filter and have no desire to use one.

I will now move away from the actual photography itself and on to the business side of my hobby. In the early 1980s, I started receiving requests to give small presentations on wildlife and nature conservation to local groups. I initially used a borrowed projector from a friend and would show a few slides, but as demand grew, I acquired my first state-of-the-art projector. More and more requests came in and, with the launch of the Police Wildlife Liaison Scheme, the floodgates opened. You will remember that I was given a stuffed badger named Sid and he was very popular at the many school visits that I undertook. He was useful when talking to the children on a variety of subjects but in keeping with the National Curriculum for science. My new badger called Bert is just as popular at the talks. As I mentioned earlier, he was stuffed by a friend of mine when I had to retire Sid and was posed so that people can see his front claws. When travelling to a venue, Bert will sit in the front seat and I often find myself talking to him (but he never answers back). Bert and I were even photographed together for a full-page article in the Essex Police magazine. Children love him and they learn a lot from just looking at him. In a way, it seems justified that some good has come from his death.

After the success of the presentations, Pat and I decided to go a step further and stage a small exhibition of photographs in Thaxted Guildhall. Pat came up with the title 'Nature Through The Eye Of A Camera' or NTTEC and we printed up about seventy photographs to eight by twelve inches and had them mounted. The exhibition has travelled as far as Winchester and Cambridge and has grown to almost four hundred pictures of both wildlife and landscapes.

To help finance the exhibitions, we produced a series of six blank greetings cards featuring photographs of owls from the exhibition. These proved to be very popular and soon grew to our present total of just under fifty. They all feature birds, animals, flowers or landscape photographs in the show and are sold at the talks and through a number of retailers. We have also produced a series of Christmas cards and feel it is a nice touch to send out your own personal card each year.

NTTEC is now self-financing and if nothing else, it helps to pay for the vast amount of film I use!

Photography has now entered the new Millennium with different technology and creating innovative horizons with the Advanced Photographic System (APS) and digital cameras opening up a completely new field of photography. I am happy to remain with my old-fashioned SLRs and slides and have to confess to being one of the few people who are still totally computer illiterate – we are now a dying species!

Looking back over my life as I come to the final pages of this book, I feel that I have been a very lucky man. I began my childhood on the farm where I developed an early interest in the natural world before progressing to Jersey Zoo and those precious years that taught me so much – not only about conservation on an international scale but about life itself. This prepared me for a lifelong career in the police force, where I was able to continue with my wildlife interests, spending almost half of my service as a wildlife liaison officer and to be very fortunate to develop my photographic interests at the same time. More recently, the establishment of Nature Through The Eye Of A Camera has given Pat and myself a lot of pleasure and I like to watch people visiting the exhibitions and enjoying the pictures. I stated at the beginning of the chapter that I am not an expert in photography and I still stand by that statement. It has given me a lot of pleasure and fun, which at the end of the day is what life is all about.

And what of the future? With less than three years left in the police force, I am hoping to remain within the wildlife scenario. I passed my BSc in Natural Sciences with Honours after studying with the Open University for eight years and graduating in 1998. I hope to put this to good use and, with international wildlife crime now the second biggest financial earner to the criminal fraternity, there is a lot of work out there. Pat and I are hoping to build up the exhibition and have more shows after I retire. The public speaking is self-perpetuating and the greetings cards are going from strength to strength. We hope to have a few more outlets before long. So as another chapter of my life is drawing to a close, a new one is about to commence.

Printed in the United Kingdom
by Lightning Source UK Ltd.
100020UKS00001B/13-54